CRUISING WORLD'S

WORKBENCH

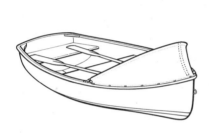

200 Ideas *from* America's Leading
Cruising Magazine *to* Improve Your Life Afloat

Edited and Illustrated by **Bruce P. Bingham**

CAMDEN, MAINE • NEW YORK • CHICAGO • SAN FRANCISCO
LISBON • LONDON • MADRID • MEXICO CITY • MILAN • NEW DELHI • SAN JUAN
SEOUL • SINGAPORE • SYDNEY • TORONTO

International Marine
A Division of The **McGraw-Hill** Companies

2 4 6 8 10 9 7 5 3 1

Library of Congress Cataloging-in-Publication Data

Cruising world's workbench : 200 ideas from America's leading cruising magazine to improve your life afloat / edited and illustrated by Bruce P. Bingham.

   p.   cm.
Includes index.

   ISBN 0-07-137963-0

   1. Yachts—Maintenance and repair. 2. Sailboats—Maintenance and repair. 3. Boats and boating—Maintenance and repair. I. Bingham, Bruce, 1940–

   VM331 .C785 2001

   623.8'223'0288—dc21   2001002879

Questions regarding the content of this book should be addressed to
International Marine
P.O. Box 220
Camden, ME 04843
www.internationalmarine.com

Questions regarding the ordering of this book should be addressed to
The McGraw-Hill Companies
Customer Service Department
P.O. Box 547
Blacklick, OH 43004
Retail customers: 1-800-262-4729
Bookstores: 1-800-722-4726

This book is printed on 60-lb. Computer Book by R.R. Donnelley, Crawfordsville, IN

Design and Production by Quantum Corral
Project Coordination by Dan Kirchoff
Edited by Jill Connors, Alex Barnett, and Allen Gooch

Dacron, DOT, Lexan, Maxtec, Monel, Naugahyde, Never-Seez, Perko, Post-It, RadioShack, Rubbermaid, Sea-Dog, Spackle, Sunbrella, Teflon, 3M, Thomas Register, Tupperware, and Velcro are registered trademarks.

This book is dedicated to Fred Bingham, boatbuilder, captain, father.

CONTENTS

FOREWORD

*I*t's been said that the two best days in a sailor's life are the day he buys his boat, and the day he sells it. However, having a bit of experience at both ends of the ownership spectrum, I believe that the old saw misses some of the most fulfilling and fundamental steps in between. For there are few things more satisfying or rewarding than finishing a project of your own that makes a vessel a little more seaworthy, comfortable, practical, or just plain fun to sail or be aboard.

The book you hold in your hands is aimed precisely at those pursuits. Whether it's aboard a 15-foot trailerable gunkholer or a 50-foot globe-girdler, the pride one takes in ownership is often directly related to the personal care and attention one lavishes on his or her craft. It's one of sailing's great common denominators, and it's something we've seen and trumpeted time and again in nearly three decades of publishing *Cruising World* magazine.

Nowhere in our pages has this notion been better embodied than in our *Workbench* column, a regular monthly feature given form, life, and considerable substance through the vast talents of a sailor, naval architect, and artist named Bruce Bingham. If ever there were a man better suited to such a task, I've yet to meet him.

Taking ideas supplied by our readers and translating them into practical how-to guides with his clean, simple, and exquisitely rendered illustrations, Bruce made an art form of chronicling the countless tasks that can be undertaken aboard a well-found cruising boat of any size or dimension. Viewed as a whole, from the dead easy to the relatively elaborate, over the years the sheer variety of projects Bruce presented and illustrated has been staggering. For this book, we've chosen roughly two hundred of his top tips and categorized them in appropriate chapters such as "Anchoring and Mooring," "Rigging," "Electronics," "Dinghies," and so on.

As a longtime voyager himself, Bruce brought to the column an innate understanding of the challenges cruising sailors face on a daily basis. Not surprisingly, in many instances the subjects tackled herein transcend the seasonal tasks and day-to-day maintenance so familiar to any boatowner, though these topics are also addressed with a fresh perspective.

One of the great things about *Workbench* is that, based on the experiences of the column's countless contributors, and brought to the printed page by people who live and breathe cruising boats, the column has always been both by and for folks with a love of the sea. For that reason, some of the most worthwhile contributions are the ones that go straight to the heart of taking a small boat out on the open ocean—namely, the techniques and modifications that can foster good seamanship. It's very hard to thumb past more than a few of these pages and not be struck by something small or large that wouldn't make your boat a safer or more efficient one to sail.

That said, this book is not only about tangible improvements one can make to a boat, it's also about attitude.

One of my favorite aspects of *Workbench* is that, in many ways, it mirrors the very qualities the readers of *Cruising World* most value: self-reliance, resilience, stick-to-itiveness, and technical competence. *Workbench* disciples, faced with a challenge

aboard their own boats, do not automatically resolve the matter by peeling off $50 bills to pay marine professionals at hourly boatyard rates. More often than not, they'll roll up their sleeves and address the issue themselves.

So, whether you have a specific improvement in mind, or are just seeking a general dose of inspiration, please read and enjoy this book in the spirit in which it was created. We all love our boats a little more when we invest a bit of ourselves in them. Consider this book one more tool in your inventory in that noble quest. If you're anything like me, as you become more familiar with its contents, you'll find yourself asking the same question again and again: *Why didn't I think of that?*

In use

¾" opaque white acrylic,
any size desired

¼" line

Eye splice

Velcro

Grease pencil

Round all corners.

Snap hook

Stowed

INTRODUCTION

My dad was a wooden-yacht builder on the Detroit River when I was a kid. He was an outstanding draftsman, craftsman, sailor, and incessant tinkerer. When he wasn't at the boatyard, he was often bent over his drawing board or puttering around on our family's boats to make them safer, faster, more comfortable or better looking. Usually, his efforts took form in wood, but metal, canvas, plastics, and rope were also common elements of his creativity.

I watched my dad a lot, so it was no wonder that I became a tinkerer too. Before I was a teenager, I was comfortable using all the shop equipment and my dad's tools. I even started sketching up my own ideas on how to fix this or change that. My drawing style and eye for small details also mimicked my dad's. I became truly a chip off the old block in every sense, except that I started writing about boat stuff before he did. By 1980, both of us were writing and drawing for the marine field, and each of us had authored several books for the do-it-yourselfer.

It wasn't until I moved aboard and began a thirteen-year stretch of cruising that my own puttering took a significant turn. Until then, I had my own shoreside shop with plenty of electricity and almost unlimited tools and material resources. But boat living presented severe restrictions on space in which to work (the cockpit or small saloon table), power was often reduced to what a little gas generator could crank out (providing its howl didn't disturb closely anchored neighbors), and quantities of wood and other commodities were limited by the space under a settee or the load I could bear during the long walk from the heart of town. Handsaws and drills, once considered the implements of pioneers, became the mainstay of my tool chest. Once aboard, keeping tools sharp and rust-free took on greater importance and effort than I had imagined. My hurdy-gurdy (a geared hand drill) and brace (a vertical hand crank capable of holding a drill bit, screwdriver, or auger) were kept wrapped in oil-soaked towels along with my chisels and saws. Except when I had the luxury of a friend's garage, projects became necessarily simple in design and easily executable. Investing three days of work into what could have been purchased ashore for $20 (had shore been reachable and the item available) became very common. Making, fixing, and changing stuff became necessary and rewarding . . . even pleasurable.

In the wild winter of 1976, I had spent Christmas anchored at Cuttyhunk Island, and was running low on heating oil. I sailed my schooner, *At Last*, across Buzzards Bay to

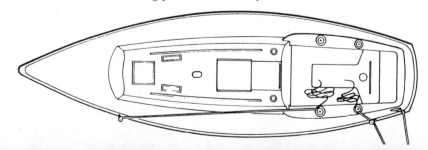

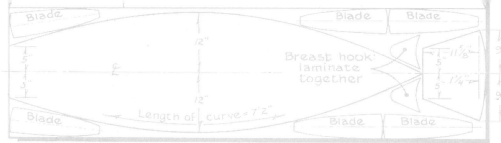

Newport harbor in a blinding snowfall. Shortly after docking, I sauntered up to Thames Street and into *Cruising World*. I was cold, wet, still draped in foul-weather gear and sea boots, and thoroughly disheveled. I was welcomed with disbelief, hot chocolate, and warm hearts. Murray Davis, then publisher of *CW*, knew of my work as a yacht designer, writer, and illustrator. Over dinner, he invited me to illustrate and produce articles, and my 24-year relationship with *Cruising World* began. Countless pages have slipped under my stern, off my pen, and out of my laser printer since then (I still dust off the old manual typewriter that launched my career).

I'm living ashore now. I bought a nice little Florida-cracker house with a huge garage about eight minutes from Gulfport harbor. I'm completely rebuilding an old 20-foot trailerable sloop from top to bottom . . . and I really mean from top to bottom. Nothing is being left untouched or unreplaced.

My garage, which is really a great workshop, is where I tried out most of the projects for the *Workbench* items sent in by readers from January of 1994 to May of 1999. After all, I had to know if the ideas would actually work as well, were as easy to make or install, and had the significant value that the contributors touted. Not all projects made the

cut . . . less than 25 percent. Some were just too complicated for the restricted space of the *Workbench* column and really needed a full page or more and many drawings to explain clearly. Other projects were simply alternatives to buying a relatively inexpensive existing product, yielding an almost insignificant gain. Occasionally, an idea sent in was an overly simple concept that, in reality, just didn't work. Then there were projects that only required a few wrinkles ironed out, and then they were absolutely fantastic. These were the gems that gave me the most fun to try, draw, and write about. Very often, a single idea gave rise to several variations to broaden its use or methods of fabrication. No submission was accepted on its face without a lot of consideration and some degree of trial. Sending back rejections was an extremely difficult task because I knew that every submission had been sent with hope and enthusiasm and had something worth expressing.

I received *Workbench* ideas from several contributors on a regular basis, and their names appear repeatedly in these pages. Their suggestions and projects were consistently simple, practical, and thoroughly explained. I knew they were seasoned sailors by what they offered, and some became good friends. Others sent sea stories with their sketches and descriptions;

many envelopes included photos of boats, harbors, pets, and sailing partners (usually waving from behind the wheel or from the ratlines). What fun the *Workbench* column was for me in so many ways, though I admit I was not good at the paperwork and answering letters.

When I draw, my mind is very much aboard the boat or in the workshop. The drawings take a lot of time and patience, and I try to make them correct in every detail. I'm quite capable of creating illustrations digitally on the computer, but I've found that it saves no time, and the resulting graphics lack personality. I've stuck with ink, pen, and brush throughout the *Workbench* series. The cat and mouse that are found on most of the pages are little friends that used to live with me aboard previous boats. Actually, there were several cats and mice that sat nervously for sketches over a period of many years.

Music fills my drawing room, and my dog, Nikki, is always at my side when I work. We often visit a boatyard nearby to take photographs, and more than once, workers wielding hammers or sanding bottoms have posed for shots, drawn by the dubious promise of fame.

They all know Nikki. I've wondered whether they brush themselves off and comb their hair when they see us coming!

The *Workbench* column, and this book, would not have not been possible without the hundreds and hundreds of sailors who are dedicated to the improvement of cruising and the joy of passing on their experience, knowledge, wisdom, and wit. I thank them all for their wonderful letters, photos, drawings, and stories. I hope my efforts at the keyboard and drawing board have done justice to their concepts and helped the readers share in the pleasure of creativity.

I visited my dad in Morro Bay, California, not long ago. He was frail, in his nineties, but sharp as a tack. We peeled shrimp over a pitcher of beer in a little seaside pub, and we talked and laughed about the good ole days. Then we walked the docks and visited a couple of boatyards, admiring sweet sheers, handsome prows, and hulls you would just love to run your hand along. We stood listening to the seagulls and the roar of the surf. I sensed that he was satisfied that his legacy was secure. A few months later, his ship slipped its mooring for the last voyage and sailed into the setting sun.

CHAPTER 1

ANCHORING AND MOORING

Getting a boat securely anchored or safely alongside a dock presents challenges to even the most experienced sailors. Our readers' suggestions include everything from a homemade tool for picking up a mooring to a clever way to mark anchor chain. And once you're at anchor, you'll want to check out the ideas for swim ladders, keeping the boat from swinging on windy nights, and even getting on and off the boat more safely.

LEISURELY LOCKING

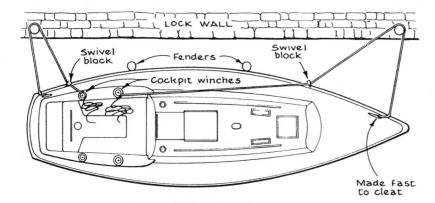

Joachim Michels from Elmshorn, Germany, does a lot of locking up and down in his canal travels. Often, he handles his 35-foot steel cutter, *Da Sind Wir*, alone. To facilitate convenient and effective line adjustment from the cockpit, especially when there is a lot of lock turbulence, Joachim has installed swivel fairlead blocks at the bow and stern. Now his extralong dock lines are led through the blocks to his primary and secondary winches, making single-handed locking far more manageable.

EMERGENCY DOCK-LINE SNUBBER

Celestra, Clifford Donley's Hunter 27 from Toledo, Ohio, was jerking dangerously at her dock lines during a storm one night. He was concerned about the possibilities of damaging deck hardware or parting lines. He had no shock cord aboard, but thought he could simulate commercial rubber snubbers or shock absorbers using small docking fenders. One by one, he passed the offending dock lines through one of the fender's eyes, spiraled the line around the fender, then passed it through the opposite eye. Once the dock lines were back in action, the boat seemed to tug at her restraints much less violently.

A LONG-REACH DOCK LINER

David Taylor, from Columbus, Ohio, usually docks *Explorer* single-handedly. This is easy only when there is little wind and when he can conveniently reach all the dock cleats and pilings with the various docking lines. To make this possible, David has seized small loops to all the dock-line eye splices at one-third of the splices' circumference. This allows him to insert the pike of his 8-foot boat hook so he can reach a long distance and position the dock-line eye on its respective cleat or piling. Once the line is in place, the pike is easily withdrawn.

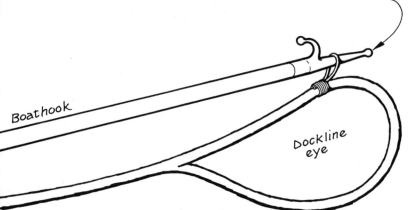

PADDING THE BILL

Bill and Carol Seger from Lombard, Illinois, keep their Catalina 22, *Free Willy*, on a mooring in Chicago and often stay aboard on weekends. On windless nights, their sleep was interrupted by the knocking of the mooring buoy against the hull. Over time, the buoy scratched and nicked the gelcoat near the bow. The Segers' solution was to drop an appropriately sized inflated inner tube over the buoy.

In addition to protecting the hull and deadening noise, the tube also provides the kids with a water toy.

PVC FENDERBOARDS

When you're docking against vertical pilings, use of fenderboards will prevent hull damage from abrasion, barnacles, bolts, nails, and creosote. Charles Rice from Goldsboro, North Carolina, provides this innovative alternative to the use of 2 by 4s. PVC pipe lengths are drilled and threaded with ¼-inch pendants held in place with figure-eight knots. The diameter and number of pipe sections will depend on the size of your boat. Pipe caps are used to finish the ends of each pipe and, if left removable, will allow each fenderboard to serve as a storage unit for such things as swabs, fishing poles, and boat hooks. These boards are not recommended during storms or very cold weather, however.

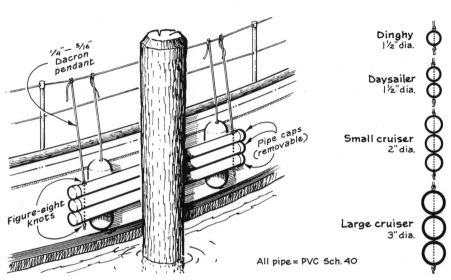

BYPASSING ANCHOR CHAIN

Stuart Miller from Marblehead, Massachusetts, reminds us that most boats use two bow anchors even though many windlasses are manufactured with only one gypsy for chain. It might be possible to switch anchor chains back and forth, but it surely will be complicated and possibly dangerous in heavy weather. So Stuart has installed a chain-bypass line to the chain of the secondary anchor aboard *Quacker Jacque III*, a Hans Christian 33. Now, when weighing anchor, all the rode is taken in on the windlass drum, and when the chain arrives at the windlass, the bypass line is transferred to the drum, and hauling in continues until the anchor is housed.

AT-ANCHOR, ANTISAIL DROGUE

Most boats sail back and forth on one tack then another when anchored during strong winds. This not only is nerve-racking but also strains your ground tackle. Steadying sails reduce this tendency, but they're noisy, create heel, and can be a hassle to rig.

Tristan Mouligne, who has sailed in the Caribbean aboard *Frog Kiss*, thought this annoying and potentially dangerous swinging could be reduced significantly. First, he deployed from the boat's bow a 5-gallon bucket with stones lining the bottom, and it worked to some degree. Holes in the bottom of the bucket made it even better. A large drogue or sea anchor brought the boat's errant pacing under remarkable control, especially with the drogue ballasted to keep it submerged 3 or 4 feet below the surface. Not surprisingly, the larger the drogue, the more settled the boat will be in strong winds.

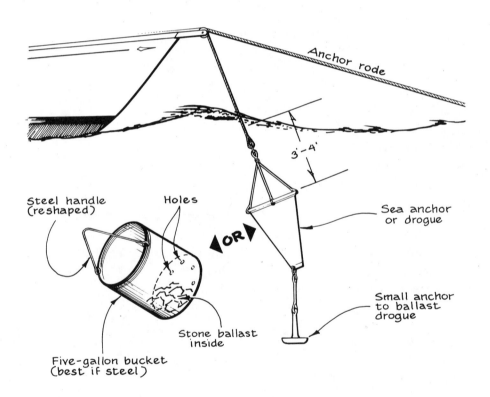

Anchor rode

3'–4'

Steel handle (reshaped)

Holes

◀ OR ▶

Sea anchor or drogue

Small anchor to ballast drogue

Stone ballast inside

Five-gallon bucket (best if steel)

DOWN THE TUBE

Alexander Malgieri from Somerset, Massachusetts, tried to install a windlass between the bow roller and the anchor well of his Cal 39, *Vita*. Unfortunately, the slope of the boat's stem retarded the free downward flow of chain, which piled up in the locker and hampered weighing anchor. After considerable thought and careful design, he had a 2½-inch stainless chain pipe professionally fabricated using large-radius welded Ls that allowed the windlass to be installed just aft of the anchor well and chain-locker bulkhead. He says that the windlass motor and chain pipe are not visually disturbing from the forward cabin, but an overhead cabinet could be built to hide them while providing storage for clothing.

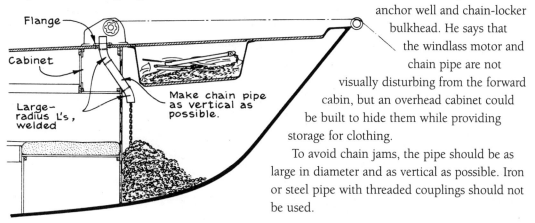

To avoid chain jams, the pipe should be as large in diameter and as vertical as possible. Iron or steel pipe with threaded couplings should not be used.

TO DRAIN OR NOT TO DRAIN . . . THAT IS THE QUESTION

Most chain lockers have only very small drain holes. Some drain overboard while others drain into the hull. The water, dirt, and living things trickle aft to the bilge, providing the drain hole does not become plugged. If the chain locker takes on a large quantity of water from bow dunking, drainage might be too slow. In case of collision damage, you may want to restrict drainage completely. After hosing out the locker, rapid drainage would be more beneficial. How do you satisfy all these requirements with a single drainage system? You can install a large-diameter drain hose fitted with a conveniently located in-line ball valve. That's what Jiri Soukup did aboard his Toronto-based C&C, *Coral Star*.

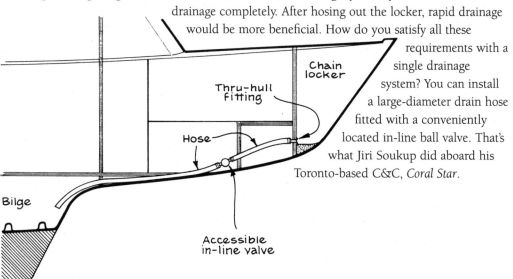

AN EASY PICKUP

Instead of using a permanently attached mooring line from a buoy to secure *Evergreen*, a Bayfield 32 from Oriental, North Carolina, Richard Whitaker made a pickup pole out of PVC pipe that stays aboard with the pendant when not in use and helps to keep the buoy away from the hull when the boat is moored. To use, snatch the mooring-buoy ring with the snap hook, then make the pendant fast so the pipe is just outside of the bow chock. The length and diameter of the pipe must suit your boat's mooring pendant and deck-storage capability. To prevent line chafe or hull abrasion, Richard recommends taping or padding the ends of the pipe. He also warns that the hook should be of a locking type or carabiner with a strength equal to the components of your mooring gear.

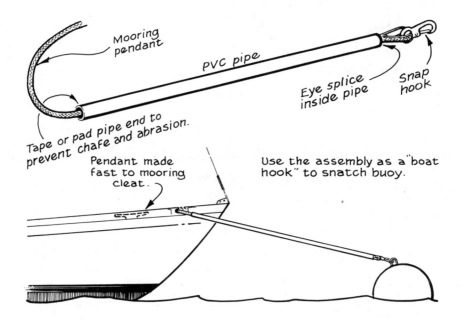

Mooring pendant

PVC pipe

Eye splice inside pipe

Snap hook

Tape or pad pipe end to prevent chafe and abrasion.

Pendant made fast to mooring cleat.

Use the assembly as a "boat hook" to snatch buoy.

BOARDING AID

Age or physical impairment need not equate to giving up sailing. But it might make getting on and off a boat difficult.

Charles Gallant solved this problem aboard his Venture 21, *Downstream*, by devising a removable handrail that is easily attached to a lifeline stanchion at one end and the main boom at the other.

The stanchion eye is a standard piece of hardware available through marine catalogs or stores. The handrail can be a wood closet rod or a 2 by 2 slotted to fit the stanchion eye.

When in use, the inboard end is simply tied to the boom.

A FLOATING SPLIT LEVEL

Robert Gillette, who sails out of Sandusky, Ohio, believes in carrying plenty of ground tackle to cover even unimaginable circumstances. Aboard *Peccadillo*, his S2 9.2, he stows two anchors in the same deep bow anchor well. The tackle for the primary anchor is fed through a pipe to the chain locker below.

But the rode and chain for the secondary anchor are actually stowed on the bottom of the well. To keep the two anchors separate, and to prevent the first anchor from snagging on the gear of the second, an accurately cut layer of vinyl flooring is sandwiched between. When both the bow anchors are needed, the vinyl is simply rolled out of the way to provide access to the lower level.

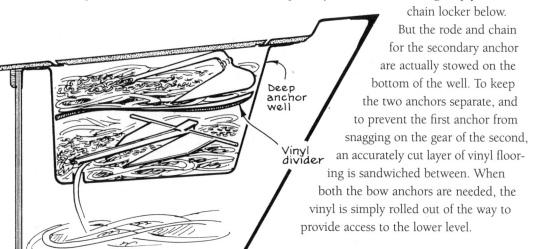

7

WHERE, OH WHERE DID MY LITTLE BOAT GO?

Have you ever had trouble finding your way back to your boat in a crowded anchorage at night? Sure you have! And so did Jay Knoll from Vero Beach, Florida, one dark and stormy night when

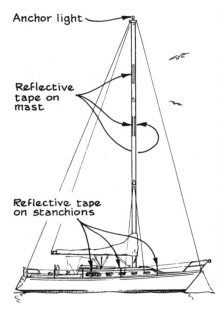

Anchor light

Reflective tape on mast

Reflective tape on stanchions

he had a heck of a time locating his Crealock 37, *Simple Gifts*. Even his 6-volt, dry-cell flashlight couldn't reach far enough into the blackness to pinpoint his beloved boat without an exhausting hour of rowing around. The next time was a lot easier. He simply attached a few strips of reflective tape to the mast so he could spot the boat from any direction. He also put horizontal strips at the tops of the stanchions to increase his cutter's visibility to other passing boats.

HOOK-N-LADDER

You'll find a very practical little detail aboard *Ternabout*, Paul Esterle's Matilda 20 sloop from Bristol, Tennessee. It's a quick-release latching system for the stern ladder that allows you to drop the out-of-reach ladder from in the water. This feature could be a lifesaving device for a crew member overboard, or a simple convenience for a person who has gone for a swim while forgetting to lower the ladder before diving from the rail.

Paul's system is made up of a pair of rail-mounted strap eyes attached to the ladder and a stainless-steel "hatch pin" or hood-latch pin on the end of a 6-foot pendant reachable from the water. To release the ladder, just give the pendant a yank, and down it comes. To secure the ladder, slip the hatch pin into the two strap eyes.

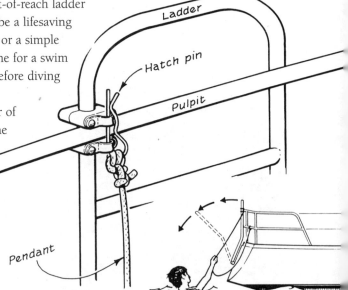

Ladder

Hatch pin

Pulpit

Pendant

STUFF IT

Yvonne and Forrest Cournoyer from Superior, Wisconsin, sail their Cascade 36 sloop, *Na Zdrowieon* (Russian for "To your health"), on Lake Superior. Winds, rain, and the high seas of the largest of the Great Lakes can be bone-chilling cold, and lots of each used to find their way into the boat's interior by way of the windlass chain pipe. But not anymore. The Cournoyers have a trick. Just roll a tennis-ball-size chunk of oil-based modeling clay into a 6-inch cylinder and form it around the chain, pushing it slightly to ensure a seal so no water can find its way below. The clay will not adhere permanently to chain or

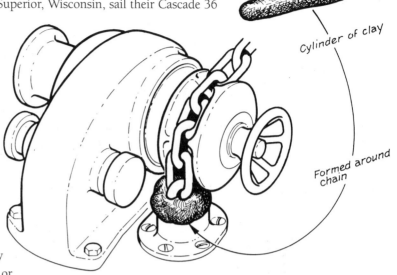

Cylinder of clay

Formed around chain

the chain pipe, and if you forget to remove the clay before dropping anchor, no matter. The clay just pops out of the hole and off the chain to be used many times again.

BUCKET O' CHAIN

Charles Althoff from Severna Park, Maryland, says his Gulfstar 37, *Monopoly II*, doesn't have much lazarette space, and the little it has is stuffed with lines, fenders, electrical cords, and buckets. So where to stow the chain and rode for the kedge?

Charles simply converted a plastic 5-gallon drywall-compound bucket into a rode-storage container and afterdeck seat that's held in place by stainless-steel brackets. He made a padded top with two layers of plywood, foam, and vinyl covering. The bucket bottom has been drilled with ample drain holes. Now there's a great place to sit and fish while swinging on the hook or ghosting along in light breezes.

Vinyl covered foam padding

Two layers of plywood

Bolted stainless brackets

Drain holes

PLEASE . . . NO MORE ROCK 'N' ROLL!

Julie Zahniser from Miami sails with her husband aboard *Sol Mate*, a Dehler 37. While cruising in the Bahamas and the Caribbean, Julie found that anchoring in currents often caused the boat to lie on a heading different from the oncoming waves. Sometimes the resulting rolling or corkscrewing of the boat was intolerable.

   Her solution is to shackle a long, hefty pendant from the boat's quarter to the anchor chain or rode. By slacking or taking up on the rode or the pendant, the heading of the boat can be changed by as much as 180 degrees. This allows the rode to be "tuned" whenever the current or wind changes to the detriment of comfort.

   A variation is to put a snatch block onto the rode, which allows the pendant to move up and down the rode. She says this has worked well.

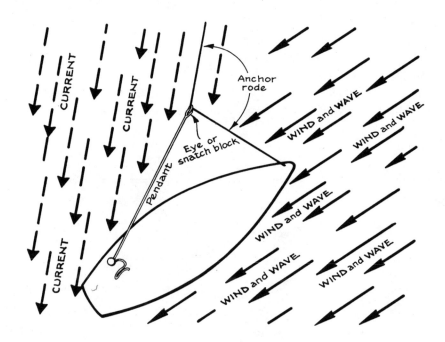

SIMPLE ANCHOR-HATCH "HOLD OPENS"

When working your ground tackle, you've got to keep your anchor compartment hatch open while dedicating both hands to the anchor and rode. The hatch slamming shut while setting the hook in a seaway could be inconvenient and downright dangerous.

Bill Seger from Lombard, Illinois, offers his system that has worked perfectly aboard his Catalina 22, *Free Willy*, for several years. He now uses the same system for securing the cockpit hatches in the open position. It only took a few bucks' worth of Velcro and nylon webbing. For heavier hatches, the line-and-hook approach might be better.

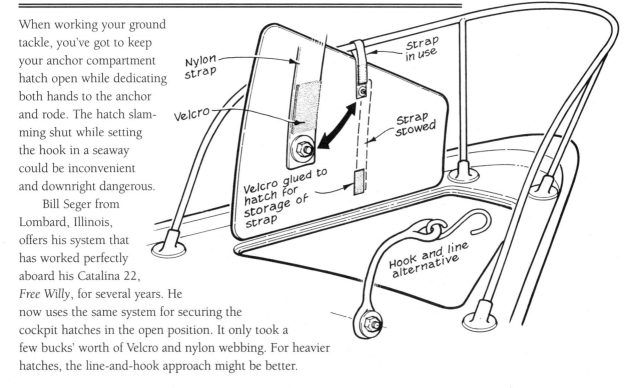

Nylon strap

Velcro

Strap in use

Strap stowed

Velcro glued to hatch for storage of strap

Hook and line alternative

BREAKAWAY AND FLEXIBLE DOCK-LINE HOOKS

Driving large spikes into pilings for the purpose of hanging dock lines can result in immovable protrusions that can pose serious risk of damage to hull and rigging. Ronald Heinze, sailing *Charon III* from Hickory, North Carolina, offers two solutions that really work. All you need is a plastic milk jug or a short piece of hose to eliminate those nasty nails.

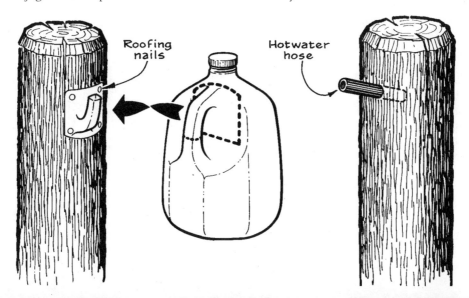

Roofing nails

Hotwater hose

Cut pipe lengthwise into four long pieces

Notch each end to fit ladder.

Drill fastening holes.

Shape treads.

Round corners, and sand edges.

sheet-metal screw

OR

wire seizing

TWO STERN-LADDER IMPROVEMENTS

To increase barefoot comfort and traction on *Antares*'s stern-boarding ladder, Ross Gilbert, from Deep River, Ontario, Canada, made and installed plastic tread covers from 4-inch-diameter, ¼-inch-wall ABS or PVC pipe. Ross screwed his treads to the steel pipes but explains that wire-seizing would have been an option. *Antares* is a Nash 26 sloop.

It didn't take very long for Cliff and Billie Donley from Toledo, Ohio, to notice that the short, horizontal stand-off legs of their swim ladder had worn through the protective rubber caps. The ladder had begun to damage the transom gelcoat of their Hunter 27, *Celestra*. Their solution was to place the largest-possible stainless washers into each cap, which prevents the pipe from cutting through.

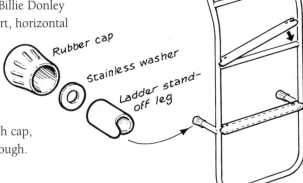

Rubber cap

Stainless washer

Ladder stand-off leg

UP YA' GO

Benjamin Platt from Sanibel Island, Florida, wanted the security of a crew-overboard retrieval system with the advantages of a swim ladder aboard his Irwin 10/4, *Bess*. He didn't want a ladder that would bang against the hull while at anchor or underway, and he didn't want to incur the high cost of installing multiple units. His answer was to splice several ⁷⁄₁₆-inch-diameter rope loops of various lengths that can be hitched to lifeline stanchions around the boat. Each loop acts as a foot rung when draped over the side. Ben's system is inexpensive, durable, convenient, and very stowable.

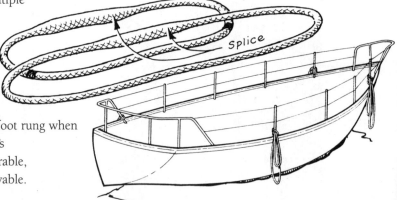

Splice

AN ANCHOR-CHAIN MARKING METHOD

Colors painted on chain to indicate depth usually don't last very long. Cloth or ribbon markers tied to chain are often torn off when passing over the wildcat or tumbling in the chain locker. Twine or leather markers are very difficult to see at night and may also be easily dislodged. For an easily applied, long-lasting, visible solution, Stuart Miller aboard *Quacker Jacque III* from Marblehead, Massachusetts, bought 2 feet each of ¼-inch red, yellow, blue, white, and green polypropylene rope. He unlayed the strands, then melt-whipped the ends. To mark his chain, he simply wove the polypropylene in and out of the links. The markings are highly visible and easily felt by hand. After several years of service, the markers continue to travel smoothly over the chain gypsy.

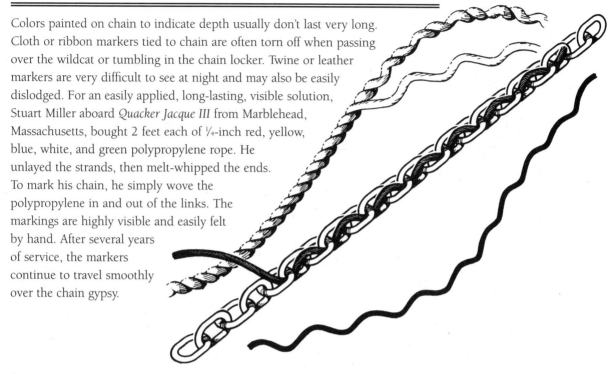

GETTING A HAND UP

Will Miller's Westsail 32, *Chaika*, from Seattle, is not a particularly high-sided boat. But if you're overboard, especially in a seaway, any amount of freeboard presents a formidable obstacle. To anticipate and help overcome this problem, Will fashioned two small canvas bags and attached them to port and starboard lifelines for the storage of a small but adequate rope ladder. One end

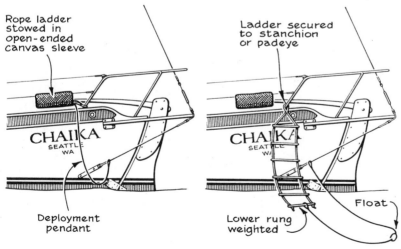

of a pendant is attached to each ladder; the other end is attached to the boomkin stay near the waterline. A quick tug on either pendant by the person in the water will deploy an overboard ladder for immediate use.

GULL GUARDS

To prevent gulls from making your life miserable (and your boat a mess), you might try making their lives miserable . . . or at least very inconvenient. By reducing or eliminating the possibilities of birds landing or perching, you will gain the upper hand over the bird-dropping problem.

Bob Pone, from Santa Ana, California, has been very successful in interrupting the landing patterns and perching potential of offensive gulls by installing small-diameter braided cord (such as that used for halyard leaders and leech lines) directly over popular squatting sites like the masthead, spreaders, boom, staysail club, and bowsprit.

To protect the decks and the dodger from gull droppings, Bob covers most of his sloop, *Neverland*, with quickly rigged and detachable netting that is held in place with hooked bungee cords.

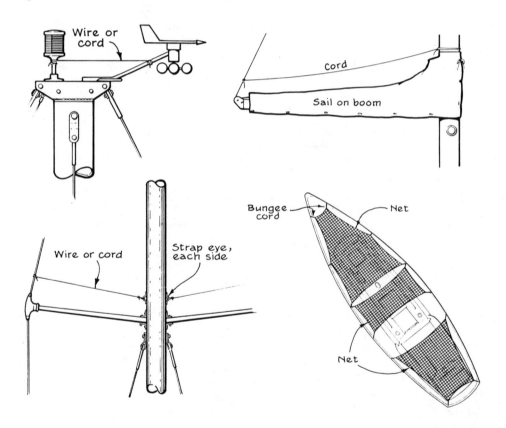

CHAPTER 2

STOWAGE AND ORGANIZATION

Few topics elicit more ingenious thinking among cruising sailors than stowage. Whether embarking on a lengthy passage or simply setting out for a weekend cruise, a sailor must have a place for all the essentials or she best not hoist sail at all. Suggestions come from liveaboard sailors as well as occasional cruisers, owners of small boats and large. From a simple solution to keeping the laptop securely stowed, to shelving in both wood and canvas forms, these ideas will help you get underway with all the gear in place.

ENCLOSING SETTEE SHELVES

Most boats are designed with open shelving over the backs of the settees. All stowed items are visible and very accessible, but often a cluttered appearance results. John Torrison decided to enclose selected portions of his settee shelves by installing drop-down plywood fronts. This not only simplified the look of these storage spaces aboard *Plover* but also added flexibility. He was able to add a small, intermediate shelf to one enclosure, and some vertical dividers to another. When the door is closed and secured, it takes the place of the discarded sea rail.

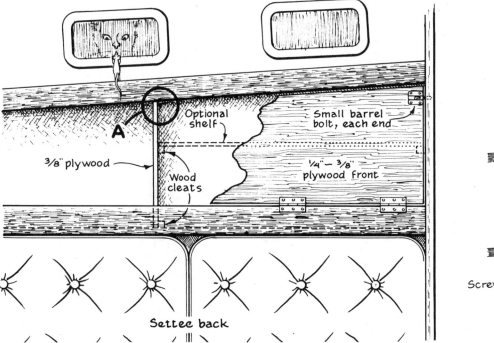

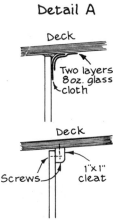

Detail A

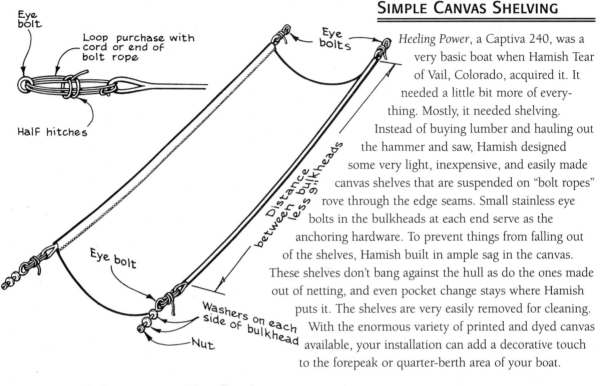

SIMPLE CANVAS SHELVING

Heeling Power, a Captiva 240, was a very basic boat when Hamish Tear of Vail, Colorado, acquired it. It needed a little bit more of everything. Mostly, it needed shelving. Instead of buying lumber and hauling out the hammer and saw, Hamish designed some very light, inexpensive, and easily made canvas shelves that are suspended on "bolt ropes" rove through the edge seams. Small stainless eye bolts in the bulkheads at each end serve as the anchoring hardware. To prevent things from falling out of the shelves, Hamish built in ample sag in the canvas. These shelves don't bang against the hull as do the ones made out of netting, and even pocket change stays where Hamish puts it. The shelves are very easily removed for cleaning. With the enormous variety of printed and dyed canvas available, your installation can add a decorative touch to the forepeak or quarter-berth area of your boat.

A REMOVABLE NET SHELF

Built-in fixed shelves are very nice, and they're great for stowing things that are heavy, such as books, radios, and canned goods. Sometimes, shelves are also handy to hold on to during heavy weather. But Arthur Lee from Santa Cruz, California, tells us that fixed shelves are heavy and expensive and actually retard ventilation. A fixed shelf sometimes takes up space that would be better used for something else.

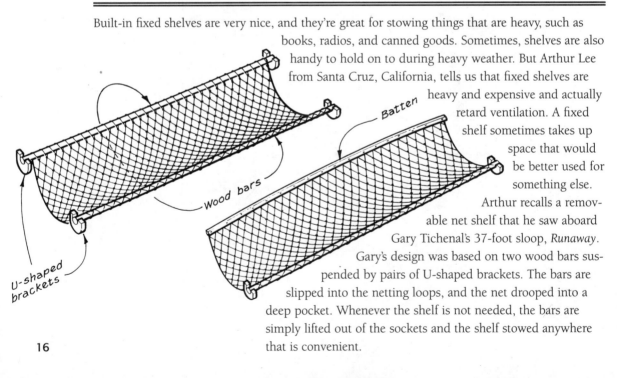

Arthur recalls a removable net shelf that he saw aboard Gary Tichenal's 37-foot sloop, *Runaway*. Gary's design was based on two wood bars suspended by pairs of U-shaped brackets. The bars are slipped into the netting loops, and the net drooped into a deep pocket. Whenever the shelf is not needed, the bars are simply lifted out of the sockets and the shelf stowed anywhere that is convenient.

TAKING ADVANTAGE OF UNUSED SPACE

Almost always, the backs of drawers are built vertically while the hull runs upward at some angle. This results in a triangular void that is rarely usable. Gerald Crowley found a way to turn these spaces into storage aboard *Lea*. He installed vertical ¼-inch plywood bin fronts using a couple layers of 10-ounce fiberglass tape. Now he has storage places for rarely used tools and other small odds and ends. Pull out the drawer, and there it is!

Remove these drawers to access bins.

Bin

Bin

Fiberglass tape

SPACE USER

There was a large, unused space between the V-berths aboard *Lizabeth*, Joe and Floy Williams's Westerly Longbow 31 from Kansas City, Missouri. Considering that the V-berth insert was almost always in place to provide for double-wide sleeping, it seemed only fitting that the empty cavern be put to use. Joe designed and built an 18-inch-high top- and front-loading bin that can be used as a seat (when the insert is not in use) or a platform for additional "bin" stowage.

Cushion

Seat

V-berth inserts not shown for clarity.

Dresser

Hamper

All units may be built to be removable.

Teak plywood and trim were used to match the rest of the interior accents. Ventilation is provided through the jigsaw-cut design. Floy says this was one of many design possibilities they considered. High on the list of alternatives was a tall front cabinet with movable shelves, and a clothes hamper.

A DRAWER OR CABINET ALTERNATIVE

Frank Browning wanted more drawer and cabinet space aboard his 28-foot Seasprite, *Gannet*. But these would have been complicated to construct, and he wasn't sure that he would achieve the storage flexibility that is so important on small boats. Then, Frank realized that *Gannet* had a lot of shelf space that could be more efficiently used. After some sketching and fabrication of cardboard mock-ups, he finally constructed several portable wood storage trays that fit snugly among the books and whatnot. Each was custom designed with separators to hold specific items such as silverware, condiments, flashlights and batteries, and bosun's gear such as knives, twine, and small stuff. Frank's trays are made of pine and are extremely good looking. Of course, they also could have been built of teak, mahogany, ash, or other traditional marine lumber. Maybe this is the answer to your odds and ends.

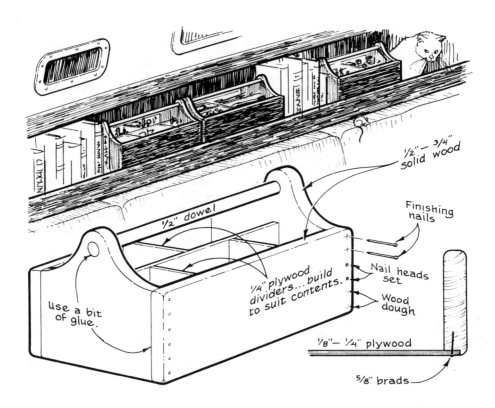

½" – ¾" solid wood

Finishing nails

½" dowel

¼" plywood dividers...build to suit contents.

Nail heads set

Wood dough

Use a bit of glue.

⅛" – ¼" plywood

⅝" brads

CANVAS CABINETS

Poindexter Johnson's Morgan Out Island 36, *Paper Moon*, sailing out of Sarasota, Florida, had lots of shelves but almost no enclosed overhead cabinets. Often articles would go flying in choppy seas or even when rolled by a discourteous powerboat. Securing for sea got pretty complicated and inconvenient with all the tying down required.

Then Poindexter got the idea of making snap-on canvas fronts for the upper open shelves. He used Dot snap fasteners to secure the fronts to the shelf fiddle and an overhead wood batten. Each front is made with opening flaps that can be closed with two-way plastic zippers when the going gets rough or cabinet privacy is desired.

Poindexter tells us that the material cost is about 20 percent that of wood, the shelving is very light and easily made, the canvas front is quickly removed for laundering, and cabinet ventilation is excellent.

1×2 wood batten screwed to overhead or underside of deck

Dot snap fasteners

Shelf fiddle

Shelf

DROP-DOWN TRAYS

Hinges

Shelf

Dividers

Hook

Eye

Even an inch makes a difference when it comes to storage space. Gwen Bylund has proved this aboard her 69-foot stays'l schooner, *Hellem Nooh*, which she charters out of Turkey. She made very shallow trays that fit under shelves. They're perfect for navigation utensils, papers, writing materials and stamps, loose change, and other things that don't require much space.

The drawers are built very lightly using ½-inch wood for the ends and side and ⅛-inch door-skin plywood for the bottoms and dividers. Small brass hinges on the back sides provide rotation, while hooks and eyes secure the trays in the closed position. The depth of the tray depends only on the space available and its intended use.

PULLOUT ORGANIZERS

Bernie and June Francis from Seattle needed more ways of storing navigation gear, galley implements, small personal items, toiletries, and various small parts aboard *Quest*, their Tayana 37. The approach was to install small drawers by taking advantage of the unused space under decks and shelving. They fabricated simple ¼-inch plywood flats to support plastic drawer organizers manufactured by Rubbermaid and purchased at a local supermarket. The supporting flats could also have been made of bent, one-piece, lightweight aluminum. The organizers, available in a variety of sizes and shapes, were modified by carefully sawing off their "lock-together" flanges. They were spray-painted to match the surrounding decor, then small, wood pull knobs were added. The organizers are held in place by small fiddle/stiffeners fastened to the edges of the flats. To access or remove one of the organizers, just lift and pull. What could be easier?

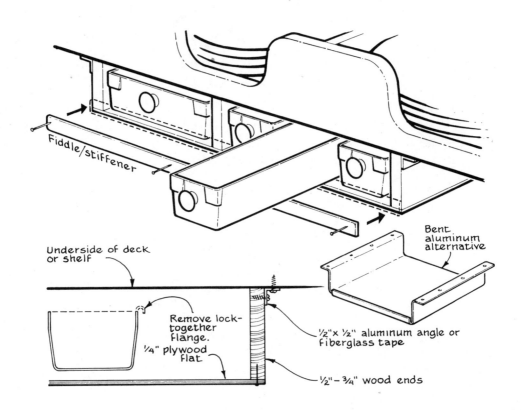

Fiddle/stiffener

Bent aluminum alternative

Underside of deck or shelf

Remove lock-together flange.

¼" plywood flat

½"x ½" aluminum angle or fiberglass tape

½"–¾" wood ends

STORAGE OF TAPE ROLLS

Sailors use all sorts of tape. If randomly stored, tape can become smashed, dirty, and barely usable. To solve this problem, try these tape storage ideas from Donna Saurage of Baton Rouge, Louisiana.

- Suspend a short storage dowel on loops of cord. One loop is passed through a hole in the dowel; the other loop is kept in place with a small screw (A).
- Glue a storage dowel into a hole drilled in a bulkhead. The outboard end of the dowel is fitted with a small screw to prevent the tape rolls from slipping off (B).
- Install any number of short storage dowels in a bulkhead, slanting them upward about 30 degrees (C).

A NEW USE FOR AN OLD STORAGE SYSTEM

Dave Drenth's dad used to keep nuts, bolts, and screws in small baby-food jars. The lids of the jars were nailed to the undersides of shelves in the garage workshop. Retrieving and replacing a jar was simply a matter of giving it a half-twist.

Dave, from Salem, Oregon, says that the baby-jar system works great on a boat but adds that all sorts and sizes of plastic, screw-cap containers are now available at hardware, grocery, and discount stores. The plastic lids are held in place with screws and flat washers.

PLENTY OF POCKETS

Canvas cockpit pockets are not unusual. They are usually fastened to the cabin end or sides of the cockpit and are designed to hold lines, charts, navigation tools, flashlight, whistle, and munchies. But Emil Gaynor, sailing a Cal 46 ketch called *Frenesi* out of Los Angeles, made a pocket unit worth looking at that fits over the helm pedestal guard. There are different pockets on the front and back sides; some have protective flaps while others don't. Few of the pockets are the same size and shape, which provides maximum flexibility.

The unit is made of Sunbrella canvas that matches the sail covers. All the pockets were sewn to the large front and back parts before the two halves were sewn together inside out. Once done, the unit was reversed to hide the edge stitching.

When the pocket unit is not being used, Emil can slip it off the pedestal guard and hang it below, or he simply places a weather-resistant vinyl cover over the whole thing.

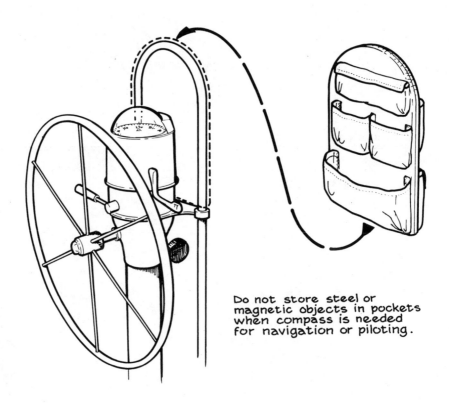

Do not store steel or magnetic objects in pockets when compass is needed for navigation or piloting.

CANVAS CADDIES

We've all seen those convenient canvas bags fastened to cockpit sides for stuffing sheets and storing other rope tails. Well, Les and Illa from Sidney, British Columbia, Canada, went the next logical step by designing multipocketed canvas caddies for holding odds and ends such as parallel rulers, dividers, pencils, a knife, and other cockpit

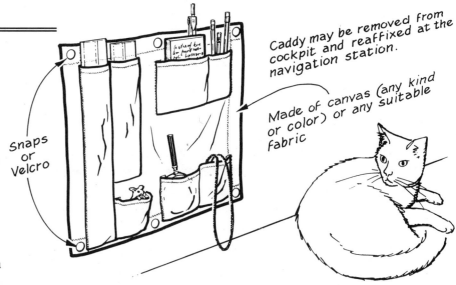

Snaps or Velcro

Caddy may be removed from cockpit and reaffixed at the navigation station.

Made of canvas (any kind or color) or any suitable fabric

necessities. It worked so well they made a matching caddy for the below-deck navigation center too . . . then they sewed up a galley caddy for the most-used cooking implements and a couple of bunk-side caddies for reading glasses, magazines, a crossword dictionary, and an alarm clock. With a little imagination, you could design your own caddies for almost any purpose and location.

"WRAP-UPS"

Before Susan Geist from Emmaus, Pennsylvania, stows her sewing machine after working on a canvas project, she whips out a few more "wrap-ups." Each one takes only a minute or so, a few inches of Velcro, and almost any length of lightweight webbing or woven ribbon.

Wrap-up straps in a variety of lengths and colors are used for furling sails, controlling dock-line coils, subduing hoses and extension cords, securing a trash basket, holding down gear, securing a furled flag . . . whatever. Aboard Susan's Pan Oceanic 43-foot sloop,

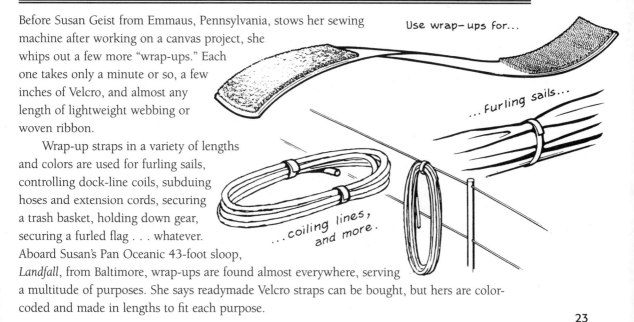

Use wrap-ups for...

...furling sails...

...coiling lines, and more.

Landfall, from Baltimore, wrap-ups are found almost everywhere, serving a multitude of purposes. She says readymade Velcro straps can be bought, but hers are color-coded and made in lengths to fit each purpose.

LOCKER LOCKER

Salt can ruin even the best lock. Dropping cockpit-locker tops on their hasps can cause serious damage. Lost keys postpone needed access to topside storage space. And engine vibration can generate irritating locking-hardware resonance. Ted Delzeith from Punta Gorda, Florida, had had enough. He decided to devise a better locking system for the cockpit storage bins aboard his Endeavour 37, *Sea Breeze*. After some sketching and experimentation, he devised a simple cockpit-locker locker that might work on your boat.

Install a strap eye to the underside of each locker top, then fasten cheek blocks to the lower, inside fronts of the lockers. Drill holes through the aft main-cabin bulkhead into the lockers, and locate cam cleats nearby. Attach ¼-inch lines to the strap eyes, lead them through the cheek blocks and bulkhead holes, pull the lines tight to lock the lockers, and make them fast to the cam cleats. To unlock the lockers, just cast off the lines.

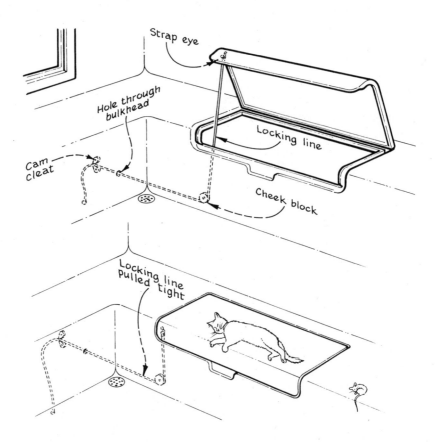

GIMBALED SHELVES FOR COCKPIT LOCKERS

Keeping small things handy to the helmsman has fostered an industry of plastic-holder manufacturers. And we have all seen teak trays, brackets, and bins in myriad styles designed to corral all the necessities for the cockpit crowd. Few of these accessories have been engineered to keep stuff out of the weather. But Jerry O'Neill from Severna Park, Maryland, made gimbaled cockpit-locker-top shelves for his Nonsuch 26, *Puffin,* that do!

The shelves can be as long or large as your own locker can accommodate. They can be made with ¼-inch plywood or Lexan fastened to ½-inch or ¾-inch ends, or everything can be fabricated from teak. Jerry's construction is shown in the sketch, but details are up to you.

You might also have some hinged berth tops aboard your boat where these gimbaled shelves might work for you. Why not take a look?

BOARD BAG

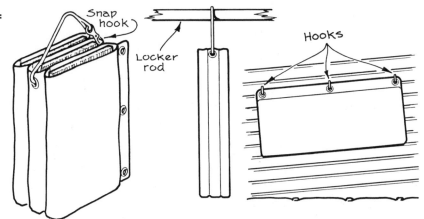

Ted Trimmer from Honolulu has sailed his Flicka cutter, *Lea,* over thousands of open-Pacific ocean miles. To provide a secure place for his companionway washboards so they won't bang around or get damaged, Ted made a special canvas bag with three sections. It can be hung in a hanging locker or suspended from hooks at the side of the companionway, quarter berth, or in a cockpit-seat locker. The bag also fits perfectly between the ladder and the locker bulkhead. Never again will the teak boards become dangerous missiles at sea.

A FLARE FOR THE OBVIOUS

When you need flares, you really need flares. And when you really need flares, it's not the time to be digging around in the bottom of cockpit lockers or trying to remember where you last saw them. So here are a couple of ideas for keeping your flare container so it is visible and quickly accessible.

Mike Freeman from New York City sails a 1960 Triton named *Goose*. His flares are packed into a plastic case provided by the manufacturer. Mike cut and bent some $^{3}/_{16}$-inch aluminum bar stock to form a retainer that fastens to a bulkhead. To hold the case in the retainer, Mike modified a nylon hold-down strap with a side-release buckle that he found at a canvas shop. Now he can retrieve the flare valise in a split second just by squeezing the buckle. To ensure that the flare case is identifiable, he affixed the word "FLARES" to the cover using 2-inch precut, stick-on letters.

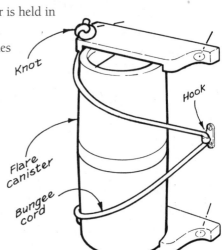

Paul Esterle, who sails *Ternabout*, a Matilda 20 on South Holston Lake in Tennessee, has an orange cylindrical container for flares. He also wanted a storage method that would assure visibility and rapid accessibility. Paul's solution was to build an attractive wood rack that is bulkhead-fastened near the companionway. The flare container is held in place by a loop of bungee cord that is captured by a stainless hook. A quick flip of the cord and out comes the canister.

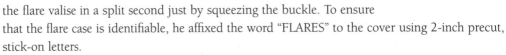

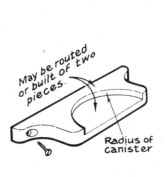

LOW-TECH HOLD-DOWN FOR HIGH-TECH GEAR

Stu and Judy Miller, aboard
Quacker Jacque III from Marblehead,
Massachusetts, have been navigating with
a CD-ROM laptop computer for years.
This very expensive gear could be
destroyed if it crashed onto the cabin
sole during heavy weather or extreme
heeling. The Millers tried Velcro and
bungee cord tie-downs, as well as
nonslip materials such as 3M Scoot
Guard, but never felt confident that
the computer would stay put.

Stu finally purchased some ⅛-inch
brass rod, bent it into a wide U-bolt and threaded the
ends to receive wing nuts. He drilled ³⁄₁₆-inch holes through the navigation table to match the
spacing of the U-bolt. Now he can restrain the computer by placing the U-bolt ends through the
holes and securing them with washers and wing nuts from the underside of the tabletop.

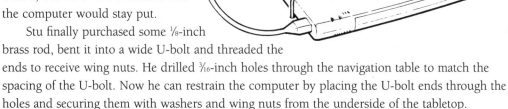

custom-made
long brass
U-bolt

Washer and
wing nut at
each end

WHAT'S ON THE BOX?

Even aboard *Winddancer*, an Alberg 37 out of Mary Esther, Florida, there seldom seemed to be enough
storage, and space was very limited. When Bob and Peg Grant moved aboard, they missed the
convenience of a coffee table. For a while, they accepted this compromise until they bought a large,
18-gallon Rubbermaid storage container. This in itself wasn't unique until Bob fabricated a top using
teak and holly veneer
plywood with teak
fiddles. Now they have
a portable storage unit
that is held in place with
bungee cord and stainless
strap eyes. They've also
gained an attractive coffee
table that can be used in the
cockpit or below.

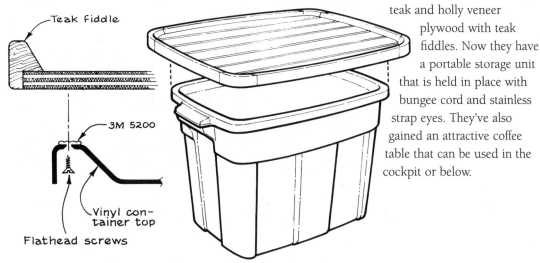

Teak Fiddle

3M 5200

Vinyl container top

Flathead screws

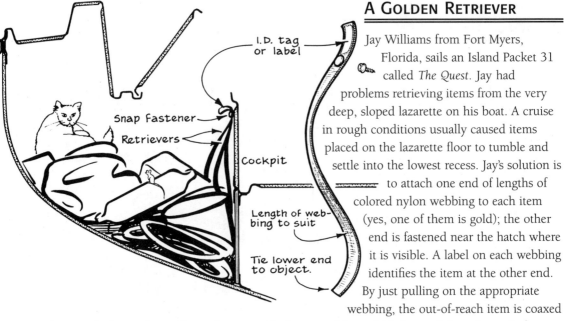

A GOLDEN RETRIEVER

Jay Williams from Fort Myers, Florida, sails an Island Packet 31 called *The Quest*. Jay had problems retrieving items from the very deep, sloped lazarette on his boat. A cruise in rough conditions usually caused items placed on the lazarette floor to tumble and settle into the lowest recess. Jay's solution is to attach one end of lengths of colored nylon webbing to each item (yes, one of them is gold); the other end is fastened near the hatch where it is visible. A label on each webbing identifies the item at the other end. By just pulling on the appropriate webbing, the out-of-reach item is coaxed into reach. Jay no longer has to hang upside down, and he quickly learned the color code for every item, so there is no need to read the tag. When he wants to pull out the hose, he just pulls up the red webbing, and the coil soon emerges.

ADDED DECK OR SEAT SPACE

Dana Le Tourneau's 25-footer, *Aeolian*, from Oxnard, California, is a double-ender with very limited deck space at the stern. At least that was the case until Dana added a teak seat/storage "flat" to the stern pulpit. When Dana is coastal cruising, the flat provides an out-of-the-way but accessible area for the life raft. When the *Aeolian* is just hanging out or harbor sailing, the flat is the best seat in the house, affording great visibility while removed from the confusion of the cockpit. It's also a perfect platform for cooking out.

Dana has seen a similar arrangement built to support a small generator aboard a transom-sterned boat.

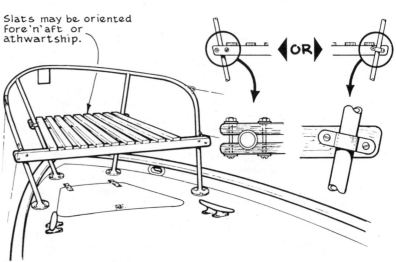

IT'S A HOLDUP!

Sailors are always looking for ways of keeping things upright or in place aboard their boats. Sometimes the method involves lashings, bungee cord, dowels, or fiddles of some sort. Well, Jerry

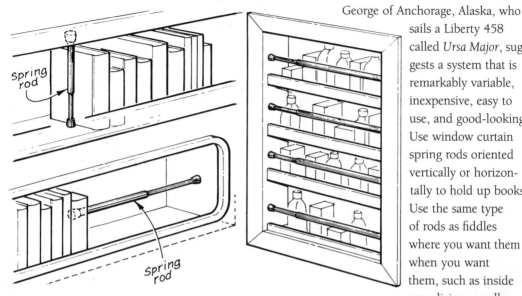

George of Anchorage, Alaska, who sails a Liberty 458 called *Ursa Major*, suggests a system that is remarkably variable, inexpensive, easy to use, and good-looking. Use window curtain spring rods oriented vertically or horizontally to hold up books. Use the same type of rods as fiddles where you want them when you want them, such as inside a medicine or galley cabinet. Although the spring rods are entirely made of steel, they have not developed discernible rust over several years' use. But if they should, the cost of replacement is barely worth mentioning.

KEEPING DOUBLE-CABINET DOORS CLOSED

Ray and Fran Locke from Frederick, Maryland, were very upset when one of several double-cabinet doors flew open aboard their Hunter 37, *Aire Locke*, when sailing in heavy seas, spilling the cabinet contents into the saloon. The doors' security had been solely dependent on magnetic latches. To prevent this problem from recurring, Ray now uses several styles of homemade safety latches. All seem to work equally well, require only a split second to open or close, and are easy as well as inexpensive to make.

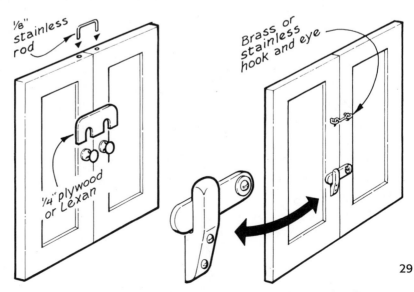

29

DO-IT-YOURSELF FOLDING BIKE

Unless you have a boat large enough to permit carrying a bicycle standing up by the rail or stowed below, you'll appreciate this idea from John Armitage, who owns *Kyrah*, a 36-footer hailing from City Island, New York. He cut his one-speed bicycle frame in two places, then slipped 5-inch lengths of snug-fitting #4130 steel tubing over the cuts to form removable exterior splice sleeves. The ends of all tubes were chamfered inside and out. John temporarily clamped the tubes in place for drilling, then inserted a pair of ¼-inch stainless bolts with lock washers and wing nuts through each splice. When the bike is assembled and the nuts tightened, you'll never feel that it has been cut. And with the splice sleeves removed and the bike folded, storage becomes very practical. Geared bicycles with their control cable and conduits are a little more complicated to fold than nongeared bikes. You can buy the small quantity of tubing you need in a wide variety of diameters and wall thicknesses at almost any aircraft shop at local airports. Various manufacturers and bike models use different frame-tubing diameters and paint thicknesses that can make a difference in fit. So, take your uncut bike with you.

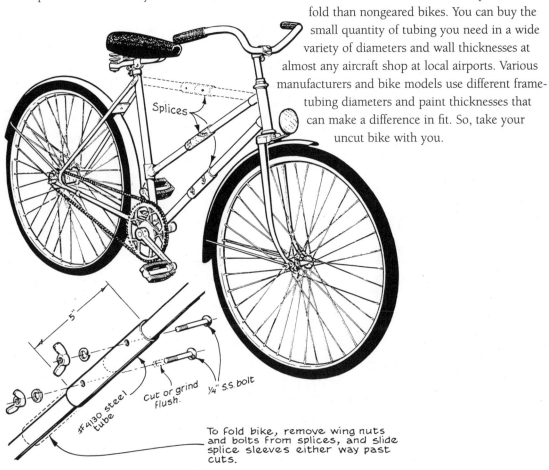

Splices

5"

#4130 steel tube

Cut or grind flush.

¼" S.S. bolt

To fold bike, remove wing nuts and bolts from splices, and slide splice sleeves either way past cuts.

SAVING THE LEFTOVERS

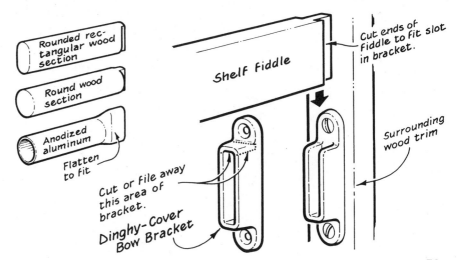

Whenever you apply a two-component (urethane or epoxy) varnish or paint, you'll inevitably have some left over when the job is finished. Don't throw it out . . . you may need it to do some touch-up later.

Wolfgang Scheuer from Fronreute, Germany, reminds us that lowering both temperature and humidity is the key to prolonging pot life of two-part coatings. He suggests that you seal your leftovers in a small container such as a film canister or baby-food jar, then place this container into a larger vapor-proof jar. Store the mix in your fridge or freezer.

When you need to use some of the preserved coating, extract the amount you require, and allow it to warm up before applying. The mix won't last forever, but it can add several days to its useful life.

A variation on this technique can apply to two-part epoxy putties. Scoop up your leftover mix, and surround it thoroughly with plastic food wrap. Keep the package chilled.

UNIQUE REMOVABLE FIDDLE BRACKETS

Aboard Irv Furman's *Neshuma* from Horsham, Pennsylvania, you'll find that he has made removable shelf fiddle brackets from stock, cast dinghy-cover bow brackets. He modified the brackets by cutting or filing away some material to allow the insertion of the wood fiddle into the bracket slot. The brackets are then screwed into the surrounding woodwork at the desired position and the fiddle cut to the correct length. You can't get much simpler or better looking than this!

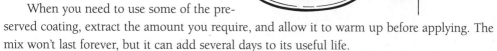

31

LARGE-CAPACITY, MANUAL BILGE-PUMP STORAGE

Large, manual bilge pumps are usually attached to a board that serves as a foot hold-down. The assembly is always bulky and difficult to stow and retrieve. But Jeremy McGeary from Newport, Rhode Island, has found a way to solve the problem.

He has fastened his pump to the underside of one of the settee boards. He says that other storage options were also available aboard his sloop, *Nirvana*. The pump could have been attached to the underside of a floorboard or forward-berth slat or to the backside of a removable engine compartment door. In either case, the pump occupies space that would have been otherwise unused.

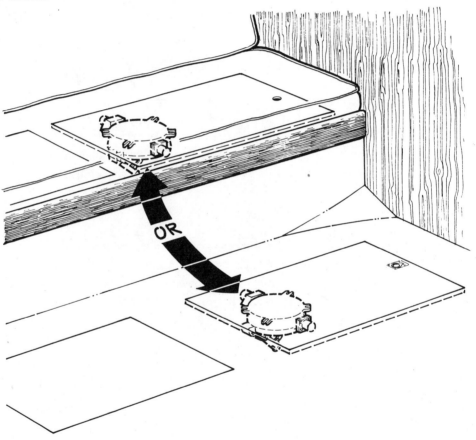

STORAGE-HOOK ALTERNATIVE

Dr. Floyd Bryan, who sails *Esprit* out of Indialantic, Florida, has replaced most of his line and hardware storage hooks with lengths of aluminum angle that have been drilled with holes. These angles now surround the undersides of the cockpit and foredeck hatches, providing increased accessibility from above to lines and miscellaneous hardware. He has also placed several aluminum-angle storage brackets on the backs of doors. Angle that is 1 by 1 inch, drilled with ½-inch holes, seems to work best for most situations. The size and length of the angle depends on the location and application. The material is very inexpensive and is available from any building supply outlet.

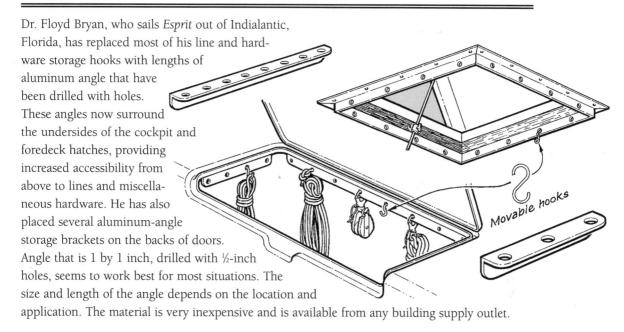

Movable hooks

PREVENTING HOOK IMPALEMENT

Like many sailors, Peter O'Flynn has installed large hooks in *Windsong's* lazarette and cockpit-seat lockers for hanging coils of lines, cushions, and a variety of boatswain's gear. And, not uncommonly, there are times when Peter has had to squeeze himself into these lockers for one purpose or another. Realizing that the storage hooks could possibly cause physical injury, he drilled small holes halfway through small rubber balls and superglued them onto the potentially dangerous horns.

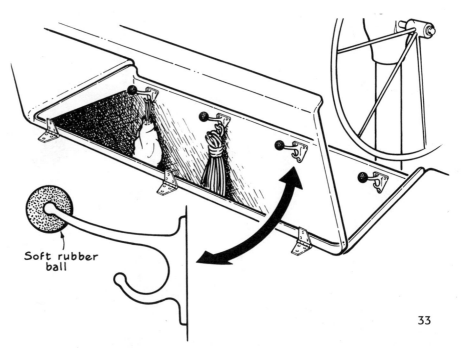

Soft rubber ball

33

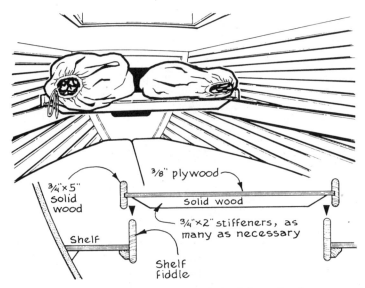

A REMOVABLE SAIL LOFT

John and Diane Gerhold from Totowa, New Jersey, used to stash their extra sails on the forward V-berth of their C&C 24 sloop, *J. D. Dancer*. At night, they had to lug the bags into the saloon to make room for sleeping, then drag them back to the fore-peak in the morning. It didn't take long for this routine to get very old!

Then John built an easily removable platform that spans the foot of the berth and is supported by the port and starboard shelf fiddles. Constructed of ⅜-inch plywood and stiffened by transverse ¾- by 2-inch beams, the "loft" can store three large bags. When not wanted, the loft can be disconnected and passed through the companionway.

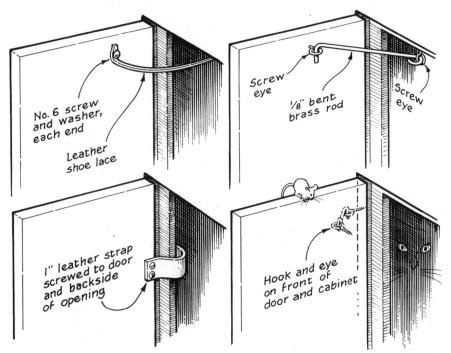

DOOR RESTRAINTS

Most compartment doors are equipped with hooks that are meant to prevent the door from swinging when the boat rolls. But rarely do we see such hooks on small cabinet doors, and Patricia Washburn from Hilton Head, South Carolina, wonders why.

After several door hinges became bent and misaligned from being strained by unchecked swinging, she went on a campaign aboard *Lone Star* to make things right. Because it was impractical to install hooks on all doors, she devised several methods to restrain swing and to prevent hinge strain.

Patricia also suggests that you check with your local builder's supply stores or cabinetmakers. They may be sources for special limit-swing hinges or other appropriate hardware.

HANDY PLASTIC-JUG STORAGE CONTAINERS

Rectangular 1-gallon plastic jugs, such as those sold with antifreeze, and the smaller 1-quart plastic oil bottles make wonderful portable storage containers and totes. Charles Rice, sailing *Tacky Too* out of Goldsboro, North Carolina, uses containers for storing small batteries, small line and twine, prepackaged sauce mixes, and even personal toiletries; another serves as his ditty bag. Charles has also made "spaghetti holders" for halyards and sail ties using the same plastic jugs by slightly modifying the handle design. The only special tools needed are a ½-inch grommet punch and die set.

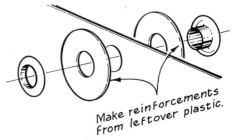

Make reinforcements from leftover plastic.

Grommets

Remove upper portions of containers.

Grommets with reinforcements

⅛" line for handle

1 QUART± MOTOR OIL AND SNAKE REPELLENT

1 GALLON ANTIFREEZE COOLANT

To help remove label, use lighter fluid to dissolve adhesive.

A small piece of scrap carpet inside bottom

A couple of drain holes

STORAGE THROW PILLOWS

Every boat needs storage potential, and every boat needs throw pillows. So why not combine the two requirements and make a few attractive fabric envelopes for packing away winter clothing, extra blankets or towels, insulated jackets, even flags. That's what Laura Hacker-Durbin did for the saloon of *Pollen Path*, the family's Herreshoff 41 cat ketch from Halifax, Nova Scotia, Canada. The envelopes range from 20 by 24 inch to 24 by 36 inch, the size depending on the gear to be packed away.

The construction is pretty straightforward. Top and bottom pieces are identical and allow for a ½-inch seam on three sides as well as a 2-inch allowance at the opening end. The envelope closure can be a zipper, Velcro, snaps, or fabric ties. The envelopes can be decorated in any manner, and you'll be restricted only by your imagination. Given the abuse the envelopes will be required to withstand over the years, an upholstery-grade fabric would be most appropriate. You might also consider a material that has been treated with a stain preventer and water repellent.

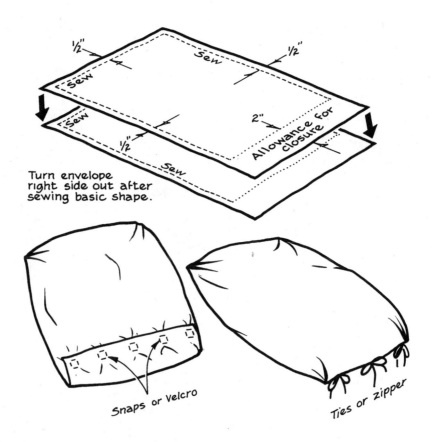

Turn envelope right side out after sewing basic shape.

Snaps or Velcro

Ties or zipper

A HELMSMAN'S NOTE BOARD

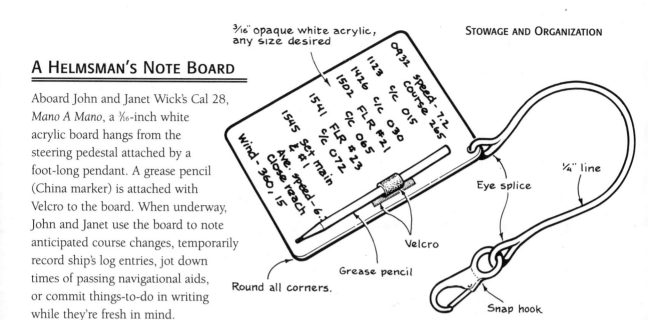

¾₆" opaque white acrylic, any size desired

Round all corners.

Grease pencil

Velcro

Eye splice

¼" line

Snap hook

Aboard John and Janet Wick's Cal 28, *Mano A Mano*, a ³⁄₁₆-inch white acrylic board hangs from the steering pedestal attached by a foot-long pendant. A grease pencil (China marker) is attached with Velcro to the board. When underway, John and Janet use the board to note anticipated course changes, temporarily record ship's log entries, jot down times of passing navigational aids, or commit things-to-do in writing while they're fresh in mind.

The note board need not be restricted to use at the helm. John attaches it to his bosun's chair when aloft, just in case he needs to write down a dimension or a bolt size. Janet hangs it in the galley for use as the shopping list. The note board can even be used underwater by clipping it to a ring on a buoyancy compensator. This is a very handy device that is extremely easy to make.

QUICK-RELEASE CREW-OVERBOARD POLE HOLDER

Kevin Dean has installed a new crew-overboard (C.O.B.) pole holder on his Morgan 32, *Via Sophia*. It prevents inadvertent or accidental pole deployment while assuring quick and effortless release when the pole is needed. Just push on the pole or float, and over it goes.

The holder is made up of a slotted, thin-wall PVC tube; a mounting board; and a couple of all-stainless hose clamps. An optional safety ring, cut from a pipe cap or pipe coupler, can easily be added.

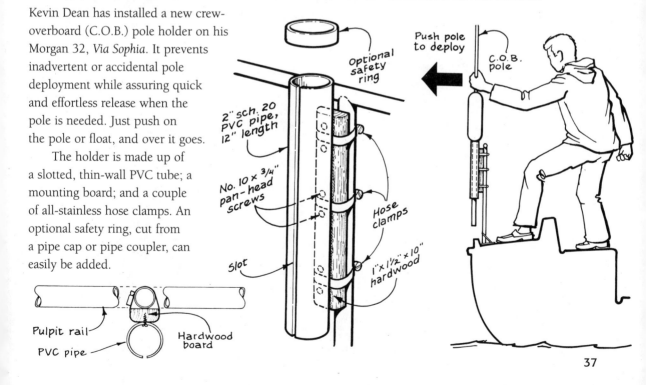

Optional safety ring

2" sch. 20 PVC pipe, 12" length

No. 10 × ¾" pan-head screws

Slot

Push pole to deploy

C.O.B. pole

Hose clamps

1" × 1½" × 10" hardwood

Pulpit rail

PVC pipe

Hardwood board

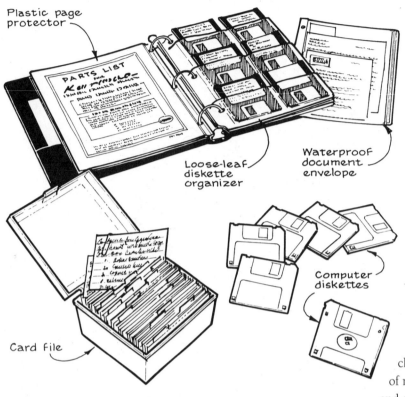

Plastic page protector

PARTS LIST

Loose-leaf diskette organizer

Waterproof document envelope

Card file

Computer diskettes

DOCUMENTATION ORGANIZATION

Jerry George sails a Liberty 458 called *Ursa Major* out of Seward, Alaska. He has a lot of complicated as well as simple systems onboard, and it's impossible to keep all the details in his head. So he places the specification and instruction sheets in plastic sleeves and stores them in loose-leaf binders. He also keeps written notes and lists of alternative parts in the binders as well.

In addition to the binders, Jerry has built an index-card file that contains even the most minute detail of every system right down to the sizes of hose clamps, wires, and fuses; addresses of manufacturers; history of repairs and service; lists of tools required to overhaul or service equipment; and expiration dates of warranties. The card file is kept sealed in a waterproof plastic bag.

At present, Jerry is transferring all the card data to high-density computer diskettes. This will provide a three-level data backup resource for everything on the boat.

THE LITTLE BLACK BOOK

For most of us, remembering names is not easy. When cruising, it becomes a real challenge inasmuch as years may pass before seeing old friends in a cozy anchorage. June and Bernie Francis, who sail *Quest*, a Tayana 37 from Bremerton, Washington, have supplemented their memories by entering boats' names alphabetically into a small phone book. They also add hailing port, owners' and crews' names and addresses, when and where they met, and miscellaneous information that will help reestablish the acquaintance.

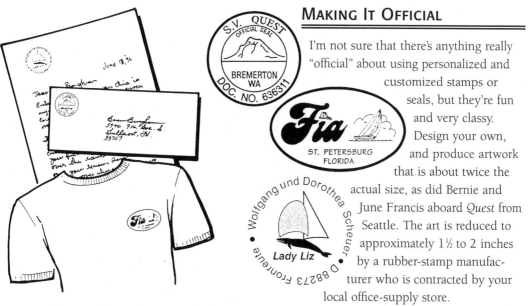

MAKING IT OFFICIAL

I'm not sure that there's anything really "official" about using personalized and customized stamps or seals, but they're fun and very classy. Design your own, and produce artwork that is about twice the actual size, as did Bernie and June Francis aboard *Quest* from Seattle. The art is reduced to approximately 1½ to 2 inches by a rubber-stamp manufacturer who is contracted by your local office-supply store.

Wolfgang and Dorothea Scheuer from Fronreute, Germany, use their official *Lady Liz* seal to permanently identify clothing and other belongings and to add a businesslike touch to ship's papers and other documents. Dave Nofs, sailing *Fia* out of St. Petersburg, Florida, uses his stamp to make his own letterhead and envelopes.

KEEPING TRACK

Laura Hacker-Durbin sails aboard *Pollen Path*, a Herreshoff 41 from Halifax, Nova Scotia, Canada. She keeps track of shipboard expendables in a notebook arranged in categories such as pasta, vegetables, batteries, paper products, engine oil/filters, and cleaners. Every page tells the quantity of each item brought aboard, the number used, where stowed, date purchased, and country of origin. The latter information is often asked for when entering foreign ports, and the notebook prevents having to haul out individual packages for inspection. By marking in the appropriate column as items are used, the notebook becomes the authority for making up the next shopping list. The book is also a helpful tool when budgeting for a cruise or conducting a shipboard inventory.

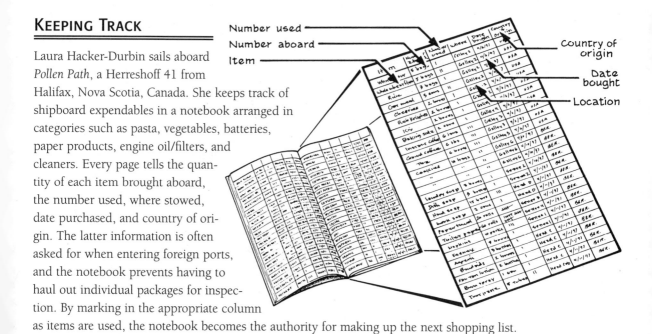

TRAVEL PAPERS AND DIPLOMA MAKE GREAT GUEST GIFTS

Greg and Jill Delezynski designed a three-panel information folder that is photocopied and given to guests that visit their NorSea 27, *Guenevere*, berthed in Powder Springs, Georgia. It anticipates the most commonly asked questions, provides the most basic safety tips, gives a few instructions, and lays out a few dos and don'ts for the passengers' comfort and convenience.

At the end of every trip, there's an unexpected bonus for first-time crew members. They are given a beautiful diploma, designed on the Delezynski's home computer and printed on parchment paper, as a token of the great time had by all.

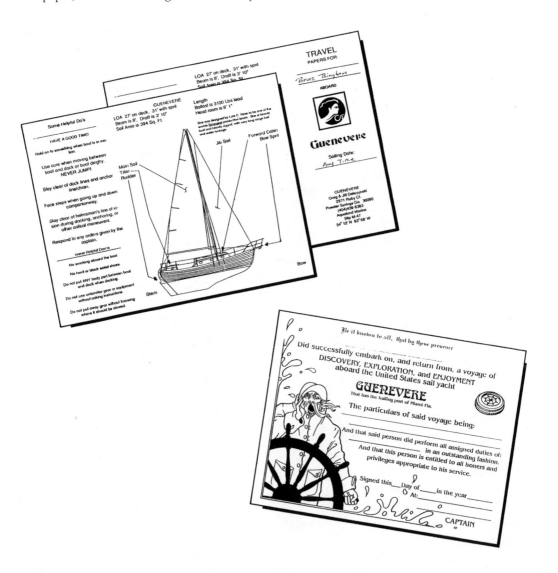

CHAPTER 3

ELECTRONICS

Even the simplest sailboat carries some electronic equipment, be it a trusty VHF radio or the full complement of GPS, radar, wind, and speed instruments. Here you'll find useful ideas for keeping your radar reflector in good shape, protecting your autopilot from the elements, and adding a light just where you need it.

ANTENNA SPACE

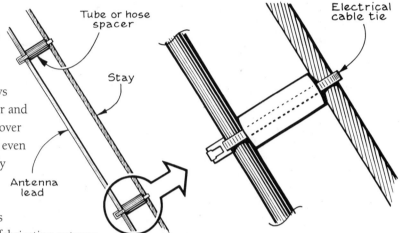

Stuart Miller from Marblehead, Massachusetts, is a radio ham. And you know that radio hams are always trying to transmit and receive farther and clearer. Stu tells us that signal bleedover can occur if any part of an antenna, even when coaxially shielded, runs closely parallel to a metal object such as a mast or wire stay. To prevent this aboard *Quacker Jacque III*, Stu's Hans Christian 33, he provided space by fabricating antenna-lead standoffs made of 2-inch lengths of thin-wall PVC tubing (or ½-inch fuel hose). They are fastened snugly to the uninsulated part of the backstay with UV-resistant electrical cable ties.

EXTRASTRONG GLASSES

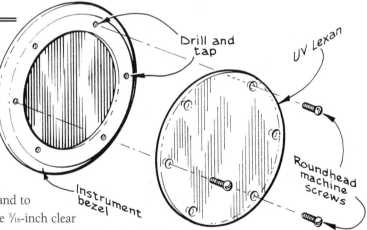

Emil Gaynor, from Camarillo, California, noticed crazing and cracking of the clear lenses on the cockpit instruments aboard *Frenesi*, his Cal 46 ketch. Recently, several lenses were broken when hit by a winch handle and a mis-placed foot. Sure enough, the lenses had become brittle from UV attack.

To prevent further deterioration and to add instrument protection, Emil made ³⁄₁₆-inch clear covers using Lexan with built-in UV filter. He attached them by drilling and tapping the instrument bezels to receive stainless roundhead machine screws. Since installing them, he has noticed that the instrument faces no longer sweat on cold days. He is sure this will lengthen instrument life.

TWO CABIN-MOUNTED INSTRUMENT COVERS

To protect the plastic lenses of the sailing instruments aboard *Lea* from possible impact as well as damage from ultraviolet rays, Gerald Crowley from Punta Gorda, Florida, fabricated a simple

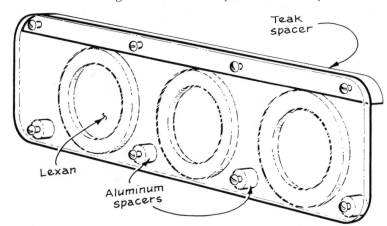

Teak spacer

Lexan

Aluminum spacers

shield of ¼-inch clear UV Lexan. The shield is held slightly away from the instruments by a ½-inch strip of teak at the top and four aluminum spacers elsewhere. These spacers can also be made of plastic or wood. The shield does not pose a hang-up for sheets and other lines, and the cabin end can still be used as a backrest.

Jack and Pat Tyler, who sail their Pearson 42 ketch, *Whish*, out of St. Petersburg, Florida, wanted more protection from the elements for their engine instrument panel. Not only were the electric components exposed to rain, spray, and dew, but also there seemed the high possibility that the engine start key could be broken off by anyone leaning against the cabin end. So Jack and Pat designed and built a sliding-front instrument cover incorporating a teak frame with a clear, ⅛-inch UV Lexan window. The frame is attached to the cabin end with screws driven from the opposite side with small dabs of sealant applied around the holes. The fit of the window in the slide grooves is just tight enough to prevent the window from opening when the boat is heeled or rolling in a seaway. A couple of small holes prevents water from collecting inside the frame.

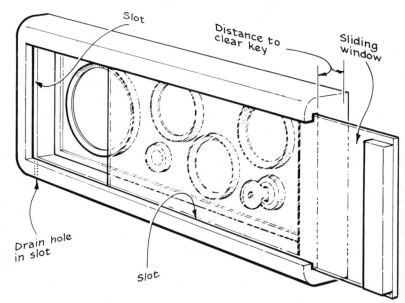

Slot

Distance to clear key

Sliding window

Drain hole in slot

Slot

A No-Hole Transducer Installation

Holes through the bottoms of boats are always reasons for concern. Sometimes their numbers can be reduced by combining seawater plumbing systems. In fiberglass boats, the hole for the depth-sounder transducer can be eliminated by mounting the transducer in an internal, fluid-filled enclosure. This installation also prevents fouling of the transducer with marine growth.

Greg Delezynski from Powder Springs, Georgia, made his transducer enclosure out of 4-inch and 2-inch PVC pipe, with a cover of ¼-inch acrylic. After removing all paint from the inside of the hull, he installed the large beveled pipe using silicone sealant as the adhesive. The pipe was filled with mineral oil, then the cap (with the transducer installed) was sealed into place also with silicone sealant. The total cost of the enclosure was less than $12.

To assure the best possible adhesion of the sealant to the PVC or acrylic, sand the mating surfaces with coarse-grit paper. Make sure that the surfaces are dust- and oil-free before assembling parts. Let the assembly stand without movement for several days after fabrication.

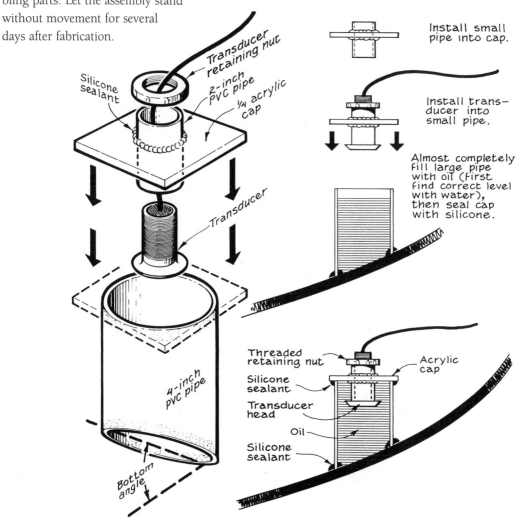

Silicone sealant

Transducer retaining nut

2-inch PVC pipe

¼ acrylic cap

Transducer

4-inch PVC pipe

Bottom angle

Install small pipe into cap.

Install transducer into small pipe.

Almost completely fill large pipe with oil (first find correct level with water), then seal cap with silicone.

Threaded retaining nut

Acrylic cap

Silicone sealant

Transducer head

Oil

Silicone sealant

GETTING A LITTLE TIPSY

A radar antenna that points upward at the birds when a boat is heeled isn't very effective or long-ranged. Marty Steffens solved the problem on his C&C 34 by altering the standard fixed radar mast so the radome could be tilted to offset the heeled angle. Steve Howell, aboard another C&C 34, from Boston, saw this modification and matched it on his own boat, *Expectations*. The parts and materials ran less than $100. Some parts had to be custom-fabricated, and the choice of metal was stainless steel.

Steve suggests a different system using nonstretch line when the radome is mounted high above the deck. Knots in the lines prevent the radome from flopping too far or out of control when adjusting for heel.

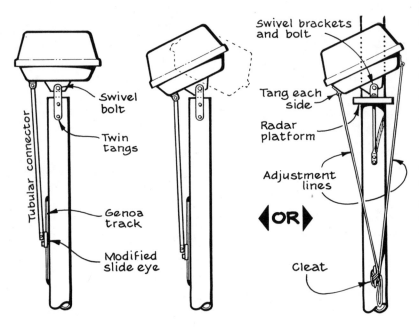

Swivel brackets and bolt

Swivel bolt

Twin tangs

Tubular connector

Genoa track

Modified slide eye

Tang each side

Radar platform

Adjustment lines

◀OR▶

Cleat

FIXING PRICKLY WHIPS

The surface of a fiberglass whip antenna quickly loses its smooth, glossy finish when subjected to ultraviolet light. Pretty soon, the antenna begins to bristle with itchy, irritating glass microfibers. They get on your clothes, on your skin, then on everything you touch. Richard Lewis, owner of a 31-foot Seafarer named *Seaquester* from Dunedin, Florida, says that your scratchy antenna days are over. All you have to do is slip on a plastic ⅜-inch by 6-foot rigging cable cover. This sure beats the almost useless short-term measure of sanding and varnishing the whip!

3/8" plastic cable cover

Steel hex screw

Fiberglass whip antenna

ABSOLUTELY NO TOOLS REQUIRED FOR ASSEMBLY

REFLECTOR SUSPENDER

Rather than leave the radar reflector in the rigging to degrade while his Heritage 35, *Kalinka I,* is not in use, Noel Lien from Toronto lowers it on one of the spreader-flag halyards. To prevent the reflector from swinging wildly when underway, Noel attaches a small restraining line to the lower section of the lower shroud. Once the reflector is in position, the halyard is secured very tightly, which keeps it virtually stationary.

Recently, Noel designed a system that allows the reflector to be raised to the highest rigging triangle without swinging or becoming twisted. Two small blocks are seized to a small wire

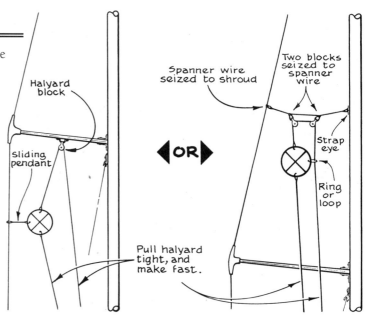

cable that spans the distance between the mast and the upper shroud. A ring or loop attaches the reflector to the hauling end of the halyard. This new arrangement almost doubles the visibility of the reflector.

INSTANT GROMMETS

Ralph Christensen from Eureka, California, was routing some hoses and electrical wires through a bulkhead aboard his Balboa 26, *Ursa Minor.* He was concerned about the probability of chafe and wanted to insulate the hoses and wires from the sharp plywood and fiberglass edges of the holes.

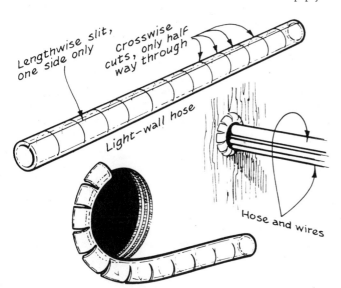

Stuffing the empty spaces with bits of cloth was one possibility. Another was to inject canned urethane foam around the hoses and wires, which would prevent movement. Finally Ralph settled on using short sections of plastic hose, slit lengthwise on one side, then partially cut crosswise at about half-inch intervals. Each section is fitted to the edges of the bulkhead hole. The size and length of each hose section depends on the thickness of the bulkhead and the size of the hole.

A PROTECTED PILOT

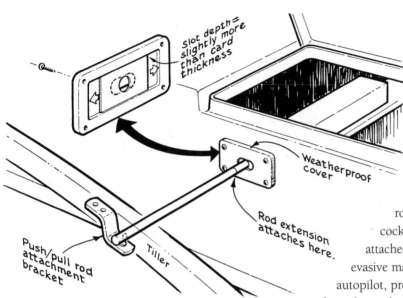

Tomfoolery is a Grampian 26 belonging to Tom Alley from Youngstown, New York. Tom single-hands a lot, and uses a portable push/pull type of autopilot that connects to the tiller. The motor end of the autopilot attaches to a bracket mounted to a small shelf inside the cockpit locker. The push/pull rod passes through a hole in the cockpit side and fits onto a bracket attached to the underside of the tiller. If evasive maneuvers are necessary while on autopilot, pressing down on the tiller releases it from the push rod.

The most interesting part of this installation is the sliding weatherproof cover for the push-rod hole. When the autopilot is not in use and removed, the plastic slide can close the hole completely. When the autopilot is in use, the push rod can move in and out and forward and aft while keeping the hole sealed.

LISTEN TO THE MUSIC

Dana Le Tourneau from Granada Hills, California, loves to sail *Aeolian*, a Pacific Seacraft 25, while listening to music. Dana also enjoys relaxing in the cockpit to music while at anchor, as well as listening to music below in the evening. A little ingenuity allows a single pair of portable speakers to serve as a permanently installed stereo.

Dana replaced the standard speaker wires with guitar amplifier cords that can be stretched a long distance. This allows the speakers to be positioned topside or below. Securing the speakers involved fashioning elongated holes in the speaker boxes that capture pairs of screws located in strategic positions. Dana made sure the screws would not snag clothing or lines but would securely fix the speakers where they would be heard clearly.

DUAL-STATION ANTENNA

Sometimes you'll want to use your loran or satnav in the cockpit and sometimes down below. You don't want to buy and install duplicate units, and you don't want these electronics exposed to the weather or possible theft.

Well, Joseph O'Flynn aboard *Windsong* suggests that you install a coaxial switch or multioutlet coaxial coupler, then permanently lead separate coaxial wires to the desired location. This will allow you to move the electronics at will. Each new position must have its own power supply line and ground wiring fitted with appropriate sockets and plugs located in an easily accessible but dry place.

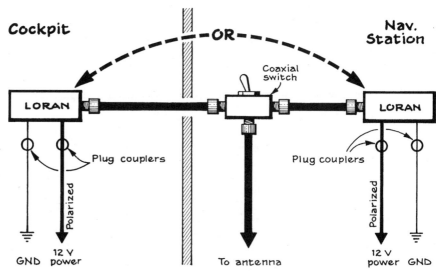

ELECTRICAL PANEL INDICATOR LIGHTS

Emil Gaynor aboard *Frenesi* in Camarillo, California, didn't like the idea of leaving his boat while inadvertently forgetting to turn off certain electrical appliances. His 12-volt panel had no indicator lights, so he installed his own. You can too.

The diodes and lights can be purchased at most electronic supply stores. You can install a light for each circuit or a single master light that will show that one or more of several circuits energized.

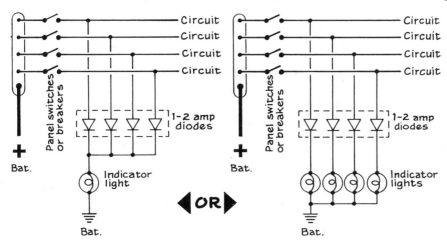

ELECTRONIC UNIT WOOD-TRACK MOUNTING

Kenneth Blust from Everett, Washington, has devised a simple system for mounting an electronic unit such as a depth-sounder, loran, GPS, or VHF that allows the instrument to be moved into its "in-use" or "not-in-use" position at a twist of the wrist. The wood track, which is slotted to receive a short carriage bolt, may be any desired length and can be installed near the companionway, near the chart table, over the settee shelving, or wherever.

Any kind of hardwood can be used, but teak or mahogany would probably look best. The slot must be accurately cut to just fit the square part of the bolt to prevent it from turning when the wing nut is tightened after changing the position of the electronic unit. If the track is to be bent to fit the cabin crown, it can be a laminate of two ¼-inch layers. Wherever the track is installed, plenty of power, antenna, or coaxial cable must be provided to allow for a catenary loop when the electronic unit is in use. Large electronic units might require two carriage bolts.

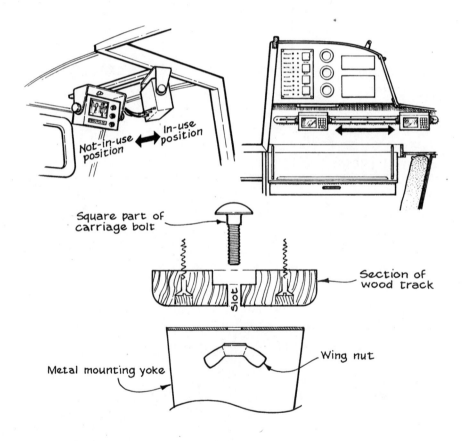

A SIMPLE, INEXPENSIVE RANGE FINDER

Piloting often requires you to know the distance between you and an object. Sextants, stedimeters, and commercial range finders are expensive pieces of gear used to determine this distance. Charles Rice's range finder can do the same thing but will set you back only about $5! As with other range finders, you must begin with one known dimension or distance that you can take from your chart (for example, bridge height, bridge span, or distance between buoys).

Using a small machinist's rule with a depth gauge marked in ⅟₆₄-inch increments, take an accurate sight measurement between the two known points (height or distance). Convert the measurement to decimals of an inch (found on the back side of the rule), then to decimals of a foot by dividing by 12. A dial caliper that reads directly in 0.01 inch can be used instead, and then you need only divide the result by 12. The rule or caliper must be held exactly 2 feet from the sighting eye using a cord attachment to the rule as a gauge.

Multiply the 2-foot constant by the known height or distance. Divide the result by your sight measurement (in decimals of a foot). The result is "distance off" in feet.

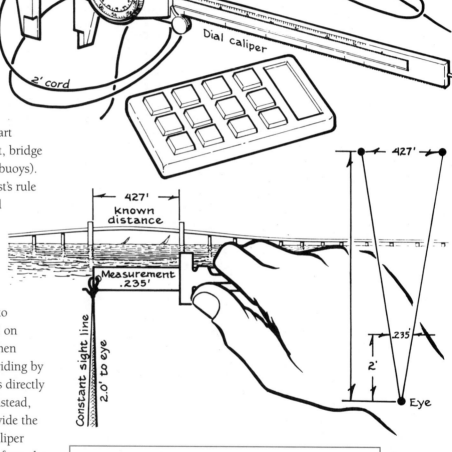

EXAMPLE

Known distance: 427 feet
Measurement: 2.82 inches ÷ 12 = .235 feet
Constant sight line: 2.0 feet

$$\frac{2.0 \times 427}{.235} = 3{,}634 \text{ feet}$$

To convert your result to nautical miles, divide by 6,076 (=.598 NM).

49

A Convenient Hand-Grip Night Light

Robert Mahar, living in Clearwater, Florida, found low-amperage, 12-volt lighted door handles at a mobile-home supply. He installed one near his companionway hatch, one near the chart table, and another in the head.

These handles are simply bolted or screwed to the boat's bulkheads or cabinetry and wired into the 12-volt system. They can be fitted with red bulbs to help preserve your night vision.

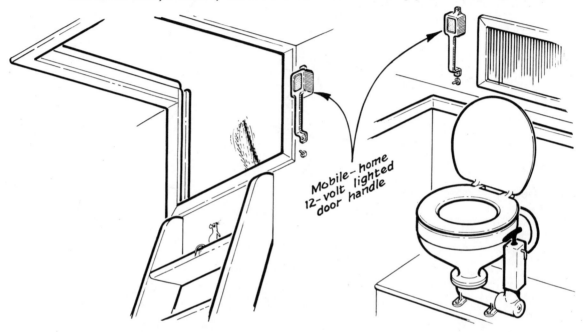

Mobile-home 12-volt lighted door handle

Instant Light

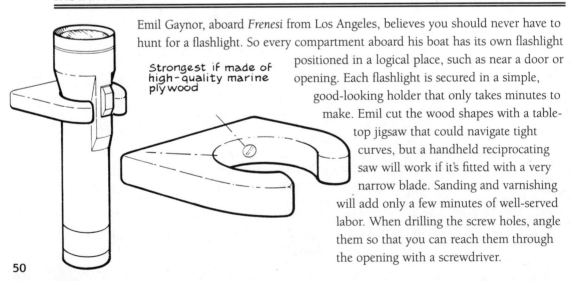

Strongest if made of high-quality marine plywood

Emil Gaynor, aboard *Frenesi* from Los Angeles, believes you should never have to hunt for a flashlight. So every compartment aboard his boat has its own flashlight positioned in a logical place, such as near a door or opening. Each flashlight is secured in a simple, good-looking holder that only takes minutes to make. Emil cut the wood shapes with a table-top jigsaw that could navigate tight curves, but a handheld reciprocating saw will work if it's fitted with a very narrow blade. Sanding and varnishing will add only a few minutes of well-served labor. When drilling the screw holes, angle them so that you can reach them through the opening with a screwdriver.

TWELVE-VOLT PIGTAIL FOR A 110-VOLT WORK LIGHT

John Vogel, from Lebanon, New Jersey, likes to have good, movable lighting when working in those tight corners aboard *Hopscotch*. Dockside, it was easy simply to plug in a 110-volt work light, but when underway or at anchor, illuminating the engine compartment, bilge, or chain locker posed a problem.

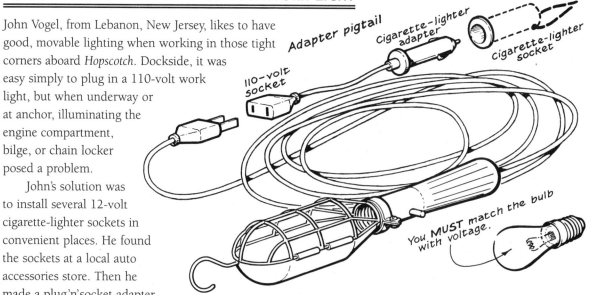

    John's solution was to install several 12-volt cigarette-lighter sockets in convenient places. He found the sockets at a local auto accessories store. Then he made a plug'n'socket adapter pigtail using a cigarette-lighter plug purchased at an electronics shop. This allows him the use of the work light on 12-volt power just by changing the bulb.

WHO GOES THERE?

Scott Kearney sails out of Bradenton, Florida, aboard a Cal 2-29 called *Mello Bellé*. He always carries a roll of transparent red "tail-light" tape bought at an auto-parts store for under $2. Scott preserves his night vision by stretching the tape over the cabin lights and the lens of his flashlight. A roll of tape per year is a lot less expensive than installing dual-color fixtures or buying replaceable red lenses for all the lights on the boat. He tried dipping the lightbulbs in a special red coating and painting it onto fluorescent tubes. The color didn't last, and he ended up with a drawerful of extra bulbs and tubes. The tape has proved to be more convenient.

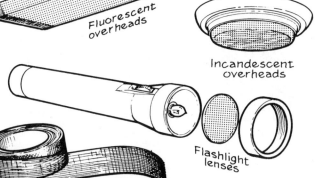

LET THERE BE LIGHT

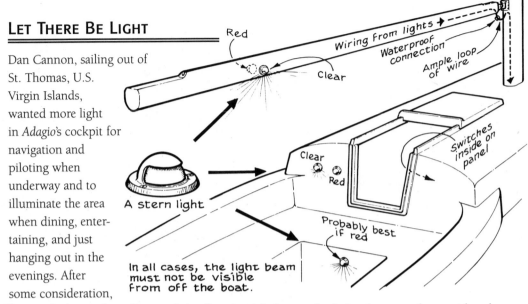

Red

Wiring from lights →

Waterproof connection

Ample loop of wire

Clear

Switches inside on panel

Clear

Red

A stern light

Probably best if red

In all cases, the light beam must not be visible from off the boat.

Dan Cannon, sailing out of St. Thomas, U.S. Virgin Islands, wanted more light in *Adagio's* cockpit for navigation and piloting when underway and to illuminate the area when dining, entertaining, and just hanging out in the evenings. After some consideration, he installed several small "stern lights," some with the standard clear lenses and two with red port lenses to help preserve night vision. A clear light and a red light were fastened to the sides of the boom to provide overhead lighting, with the wiring exiting at the gooseneck, then entering the mast. A matching pair of lights has been installed in the cabin end to illuminate the bridge deck and forward end of the port seat. Switches for the lights are located out of the weather just inside the companionway. Dan is careful not to use the boom-mounted lights when at anchor to avoid confusing passing boats.

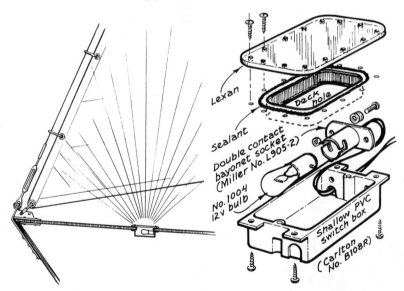

Lexan

Deck hole

Sealant

Double contact bayonet socket (Miller No. L905-2)

No. 1004 12v bulb

Shallow PVC switch box

(Carlton No. B10BR)

LIGHT AHEAD

Joe Becker from Tulsa, Oklahoma, wanted to light up the headsails at night aboard his Catalina 22, *Luff Affair*. This would be helpful on the foredeck when raising and lowering sails and would also help him "read" the jib when sailing in the dark. He cut a small hole through the foredeck, sealed the edge with an epoxy putty, then covered the aperture with Lexan. Under the deck, Joe installed a homemade fixture that allows light to shine upward through a small hole. The light switch was placed within reach of the cockpit. When the light is on, no beam can be seen by other boats nor can direct light impair the night vision of the helmsperson. Recently, Joe added a rheostat so he can adjust the light's intensity.

Chapter 4

RIGGING

Seamanship is a matter of pride among many sailors, and nowhere on the boat is this art more important than in the rigging. Woe to the sailor who doesn't know his way around a good splice, who fails to recognize that chafe is the enemy, or who doesn't keep the sails' control lines in top working order at all times. Our readers share their tips for such concerns as changing halyards, doing in-line splices, keeping mast grooves clear, even raising the ensign.

AN IN-LINE EYE SPLICE FOR BRAIDED LINE

Two-time national Catalina 22 champion, Joe Becker, has an interesting method for attaching the headsail sheets aboard *Luff Affair*. He uses what he calls a "Brummel" eye splice. It's strong, light, very easy to make, and does not require a shackle attachment to the sail.

The sketches clearly show how the splice is made. You need not have mastered splicing braided line, but you do require a fid that is two sizes larger than the line diameter.

The Brummel splice can be used in all sorts of other ways: for dinghy-lifting bridles, double-ended pole guys, lazy jacks, various dock lines, or almost any application that requires the eye to be positioned somewhere other than at the end of the line.

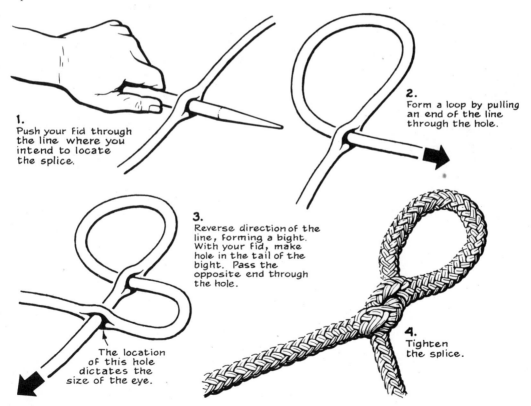

1.
Push your fid through the line where you intend to locate the splice.

2.
Form a loop by pulling an end of the line through the hole.

3.
Reverse direction of the line, forming a bight. With your fid, make hole in the tail of the bight. Pass the opposite end through the hole.

The location of this hole dictates the size of the eye.

4.
Tighten the splice.

BAG IT

It really bothered Dick and Kay Guerra from Elmhurst, Illinois, to leave their roller-furling sheets lying on the deck of their Newport 31, *Mind Mender*, or suspended from the headsail, exposed to the destructive effects of sunlight, dirt and pollution, and rain. To solve this, they purchased a small sailbag and installed a couple of brass drainage grommets. Leaving them attached to the sail, the sheets are coiled and placed into the bag, which is lashed to the pulpit or tied to the headsail clew. This has worked so well to keep their expensive lines in tip-top shape that they now bag their halyard, mainsheet, and other coils before leaving at the end of a sailing day.

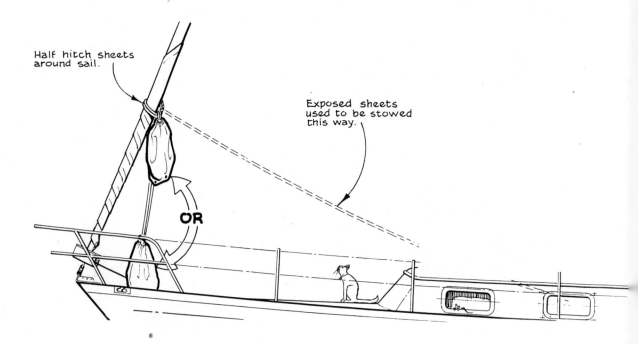

Half hitch sheets around sail.

OR

Exposed sheets used to be stowed this way.

AT THE READY

Some owners have installed various types of line hooks, line baskets, and Velcro line holders for securing rope coils. Can it be simpler? Lee Johnson thinks so. Aboard *Freewind*, his C&C 40 from Everett, Washington, the solution for keeping coils neatly at the ready is a simple loop about a

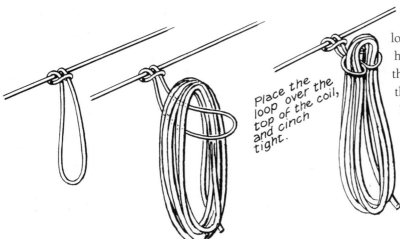

foot long made of small stuff. First, secure the loop to anything at all (a handrail, lifeline, cleat), then pull the loop through the opening of the coil. Lastly, place the loop over the top of the coil and snug it down. You won't believe it until you try it, but it works great.

Place the loop over the top of the coil, and cinch tight.

IT'S A CINCH

Many cruising boats are using some form of lazy jacks as a boom furling system. Once a sail has been dropped and loosely gathered by the lazy jacks, what next? Some sailors compress and tie the canvas bundle with "gaskets," while others constrict the sail with loops of bungee cord. But how about the idea used aboard Ray Freeman's Corbin 39, *Compass Rose*, from Winthrop, Massachusetts: a bronze piston hank is whipped to all the lazy-jack falls on one side of the boom only. Once the sail has been dropped, the hanks are simply snapped to the opposing falls. That's it . . . nothing more.

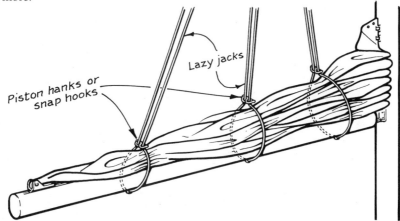

Lazy jacks

Piston hanks or snap hooks

FAKING IT

When a line is coiled in neat-looking circular loops or flemished as a tightly spiraled flat mat, as is often done with dock lines, twists and kinks result when the line is pulled out for use. Sheets, halyards, and guys that have been circularly coiled for the sake of neatness will rarely run free and will usually hang up at blocks or fairleads. This is more true with braided line than with laid line.

Ralph Stetson from Concord, Massachusetts, reminds us that faking (or flaking) lines is the correct and safer way of coiling lines that must be available for immediate use. Faking simply involves coiling a line as a series of figure eights instead of loops. The line will conform to the figure eight very naturally, and you won't have to twist the line with your fingers as required when making a circular coil.

Circular and flemish coils look shipshape when your boat is dockside or resting at anchor but are not very practical when underway.

A variation of the figure-eight fake is the laying out of a line on deck using elongated eights. This is ideal when you intend to run out a lot of anchor rode or a towline very quickly.

Running end

Tail

CLEAT GUARD

If you've ever had a sheet snag on a cleat in the middle of a tack when maneuvering in tight quarters or when single-handing at night, you know how dangerous this can be. And it isn't just sheets that get hung up; any snagged line can get you in a heap of trouble at the most inconvenient time.

Dick Vale from Punta Gorda, Florida, had his share of trouble too until he perfected his cleat hang-up preventer. It's just two wood wedges held together by a continuous loop of bungee cord that prevents lines (and toes) from getting caught under the cleat horns. He has made six of them for his Sabre 34, *Nike*. He is sure these will work just as well aboard your own boat.

SLACK THE JACK, MACK

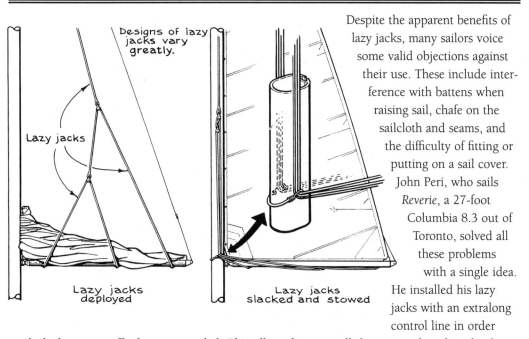

Despite the apparent benefits of lazy jacks, many sailors voice some valid objections against their use. These include interference with battens when raising sail, chafe on the sailcloth and seams, and the difficulty of fitting or putting on a sail cover. John Peri, who sails *Reverie*, a 27-foot Columbia 8.3 out of Toronto, solved all these problems with a single idea. He installed his lazy jacks with an extralong control line in order to slack them way off when not needed. This allows him to pull the port and starboard sides forward to the mast where he connects them together with a toggled bungee (or a bungee with small hooks at each end). John deploys the lazy jacks only when actually dousing sail. At other times, the jacks are stowed.

REINFORCED CANVAS GROMMETS

Emil Gaynor from Camarillo, California, offers this simple technique for reinforcing and reducing edge chafe of canvas and grommets. Cut vinyl or thin leather washers about ½ inch larger than the grommet, then punch the holes with your grommet punch. Sandwich the canvas with the washers when installing the grommet.

The washers can be round or cut as decorative stars. Plastic lids from canned food products such as coffee are a source for the vinyl.

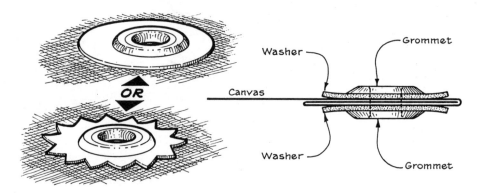

FASCINATING FASTENINGS

Mary Richards from Bellaire, Michigan, has come up with an interesting method of fastening canvas closures such as sail covers. She calls these little doohickeys "tadpole toggles." They're simply made out of small braided line and a little bit of waxed twine.

Double over a short length of line, then sew the two sides together to form a "tail" until a small loop, or "head," is left open at one end. Heat-fuse the end of the tail. Now whipstitch the neck of the tadpole to the side of the canvas directly opposite its respective grommet, being sure to leave the head and tail free.

To use the tadpole toggle, just pass the head through the canvas grommet, then stick the tail through the opening in the head. It's simple and inexpensive, but it really works.

TERMINAL TUBING

Sharon and Richard Gunzel from Darien, Connecticut, noticed that moisture had penetrated the original lifeline-wire coatings and terminals aboard their Pearson 28, *Genesis*. The resulting dangerous corrosion and unsightly rust led them to replace the lifelines. Richard decided to use a manually crimped style of hardware. To protect the new fittings, the Gunzels slid short lengths of clear heat-shrink tubing onto the wire before installing the terminals. Once the terminals were crimped, the tubing was slid over the end of the terminal and shrunk with an LP barbecue lighter. Now, every lifeline terminal has a waterproof plastic sleeve that prevents moisture from seeping into the terminal and wire.

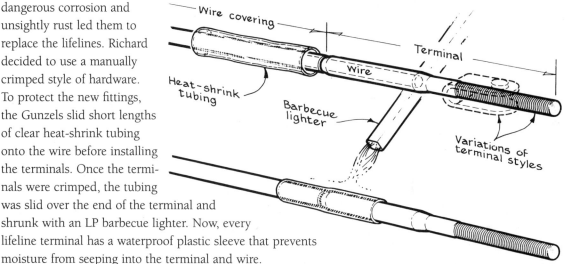

A NIFTY SAIL-TIE ORGANIZER

If you don't have an automatic furling system, you might try John Mellor's method (Wester Ross, Scotland) for keeping his sail ties together, in correct order and location. This gadget can be left on the boom for day sails, or removed and stowed for long trips.

You can buy a ready-made bungee cord from a bike shop or make your own. For the rope, either laid or braided line will do.

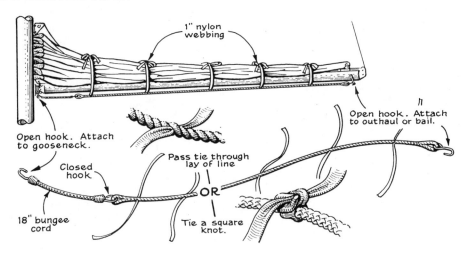

CLEAN, SELF-WHIPPING LINE CUTTING

You might come across Michael Bishop in Kemah, Texas, armed with a propane torch and an old hacksaw blade. No, he's not repelling boarders. It's the way he cuts Dacron or nylon line aboard *Princesse Elena*.

One end of the blade is heated orange-hot, then he melts through three-quarters of the line with the smooth side down. After reheating the blade, he rotates the line and melts through the opposite side. He wears work gloves to prevent burning his hands. He says that an old wood-handled kitchen knife would work just as well.

Because the heating and slow cooling of the steel makes the blade very bendable, quenching in water will restore its temper.

A hot blade is also the cleanest way to whip fraying line ends because it doesn't leave the awful-looking black goop that results when you melt line with flame.

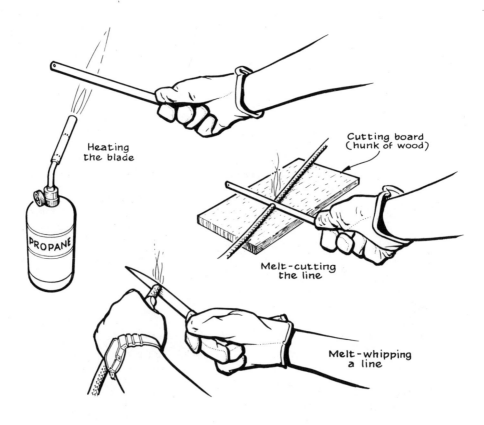

Heating the blade

Cutting board (chunk of wood)

Melt-cutting the line

Melt-whipping a line

PROPANE

A FANTASTIC IN-LINE CLEAT

Charles Rice from Goldsboro, North Carolina, suggests a simple little gizmo so nifty and practical that you'll want to make a bunch of them. It can be made of aluminum plate, Lexan, laminated phenolic, or a good grade of marine plywood. The drawings show all the necessary details and dimensions that apply to various line sizes. These cleats can be used for myriad purposes: fender adjusters, cleating tackles, adjusting dock line and dinghy painters, cleating storage tie-downs, awning and Bimini adjusters, even sail gaskets.

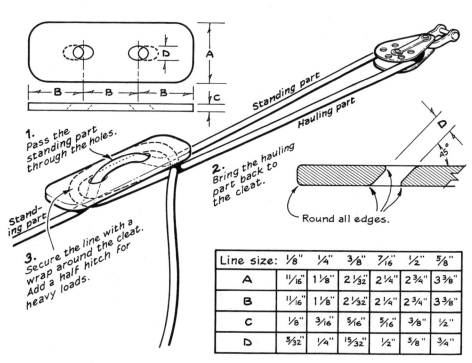

1. Pass the standing part through the holes.

2. Bring the hauling part back to the cleat.

3. Secure the line with a wrap around the cleat. Add a half hitch for heavy loads.

Round all edges.

Line size:	⅛"	¼"	⅜"	⁷⁄₁₆"	½"	⅝"
A	¹¹⁄₁₆"	1⅛"	2¹⁄₃₂"	2¼"	2¾"	3⅜"
B	¹¹⁄₁₆"	1⅛"	2¹⁄₃₂"	2¼"	2¾"	3⅜"
C	⅛"	³⁄₁₆"	⁵⁄₁₆"	⁵⁄₁₆"	⅜"	½"
D	⁵⁄₃₂"	¼"	¹⁵⁄₃₂"	½"	⅝"	¾"

CUTTING RIGGING WIRE

Wolfgang Scheuer, a professional charter captain from Fronreute, Germany, has a special trick to make cutting rigging wire with a hacksaw easier. To prevent the individual wire strands from shifting, and to keep the wire cable perfectly round while cutting, he wraps several tight turns of seizing wire around the cable on each side of the cut location. The finished cut is accurate, clean, and straight.

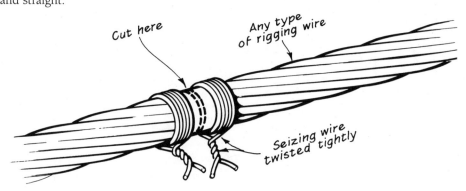

Cut here

Any type of rigging wire

Seizing wire twisted tightly

NO-SNAG MAST STEPS

Mast steps are useful on cruising boats for going aloft to check rigging or for better eyeball piloting. But halyards can get fouled on them, and overlapping headsails may snag on them at the most inopportune times. Here's a solution that is effective, durable, and better looking than most other schemes.

Drill two ³⁄₁₆-inch holes through the outboard end of each step (best done on a drill press). After installing the mast steps, reeve ¹⁄₁₆-inch vinyl-covered stainless rigging wire through the holes. Thimbled nicopress eyes are made in each end of each wire, then attached to the mast with small stainless strap eyes. Because the small-diameter wire will stretch and loosen over time, the lower ends are best seized to the strap eyes so they can be periodically retightened.

A less expensive alternative to the vinyl-covered wire is ⅛-inch Dacron leader cord purchased from your sailmaker. However, it will have to be replaced quite often because of chafe at the step holes.

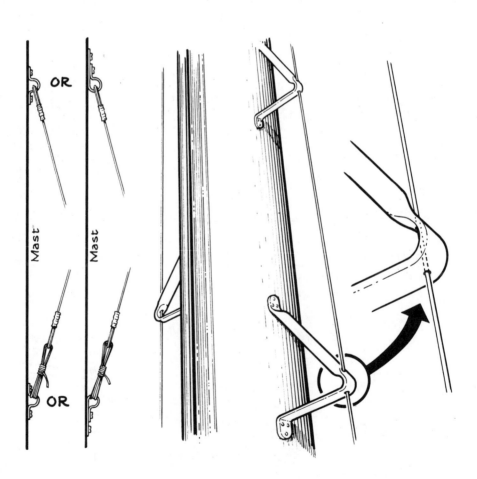

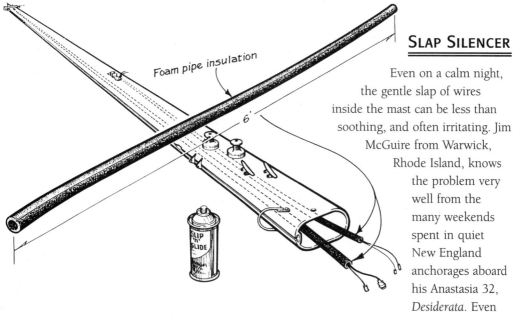

Foam pipe insulation

SLAP SILENCER

Even on a calm night, the gentle slap of wires inside the mast can be less than soothing, and often irritating. Jim McGuire from Warwick, Rhode Island, knows the problem very well from the many weekends spent in quiet New England anchorages aboard his Anastasia 32, *Desiderata*. Even during the calmest weather at dockside, the magnified rap-slap-rap of cables and antennae against the walls of the aluminum extrusion can be like water torture when you're trying to get some shut-eye. Jim was determined to put a stop to it and, by golly, he did! Before restepping the mast after the long winter layup, Jim slid lengths of foam pipe insulation, one after another, along each group of wires. A shot of Teflon spray lubricant inside each foam section simplified the job.

A SIMPLE CRUTCH FOR SMALL-BOAT MAST STOWAGE

Charles Gallant from Beach Haven Park, New Jersey, owns a Venture 21 called *Downstream*. Its mast is tabernacle mounted on the cabintop, so it is quite easy for Charles to lower it with the help of another person. Before dropping the rig, Charles sets up a rather ingenious self-standing mast crutch that simply slips under the port and starboard cockpit cleats. When down, the mast serves as the supporting strongback for the boat's winter cover.

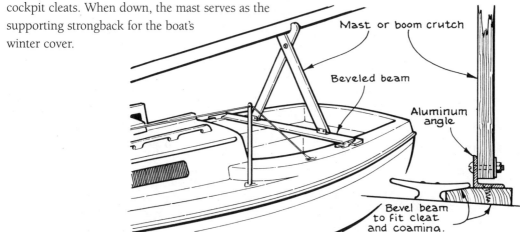

Mast or boom crutch

Beveled beam

Aluminum angle

Bevel beam to fit cleat and coaming.

ADD A STAYSAIL

There are times when some sloops do a little better when flying an inner jib: using a light-reaching staysail with a large, overlapping headsail; hoisting a storm staysail with a double-reefed main; or going to weather in rough seas with a yankee and jib staysail. Every boat is different, of course, but all sailing vessels seem to appreciate sail-plan flexibility.

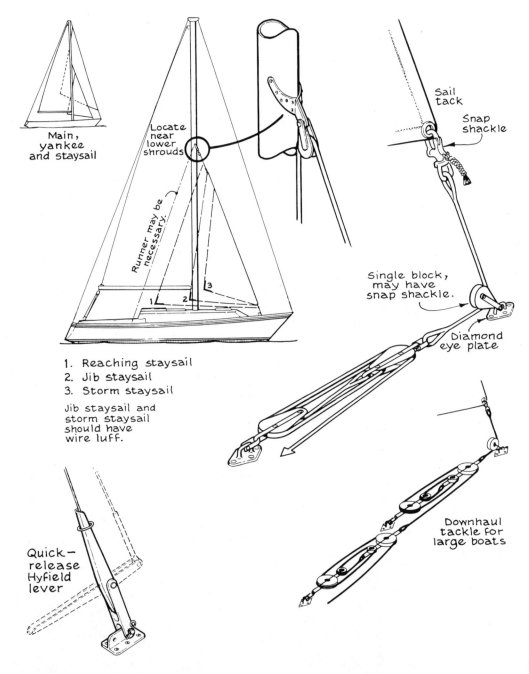

Main, yankee and staysail

Locate near lower shrouds

Runner may be necessary.

1. Reaching staysail
2. Jib staysail
3. Storm staysail

Jib staysail and storm staysail should have wire luff.

Quick-release Hyfield lever

Sail tack

Snap shackle

Single block, may have snap shackle.

Diamond eye plate

Downhaul tackle for large boats

Dana Le Tourneau, from Granada Hills, California, uses a rigging system for setting different staysails aboard *Aeolian*, a Pacific Seacraft 25. Dana installed a hound for a staysail halyard on the mast near the intersection of the lower shrouds, placed a diamond-eye plate on the foredeck for the staysail tack, and, finally, attached a tackle to the diamond eye as a means of fastening the staysail tack and tightening or adjusting the staysail luff. Dana has also installed a downhaul that can be snapped to the halyard or head of the sail to aid dousing in heavy weather.

Whenever strong winds are forecast, Dana sets up the staysail rigging with the stormsail attached and ready to go but bundled and stopped on the foredeck. The storm staysail has been built with a wire luff to withstand a lot of tension, but lighter sails have only taped luffs.

Before installing your own staysail system, consult with your sailmaker or local rigging shop to determine the best location of fittings. If the diamond-eye plate on the foredeck cannot be installed very close, or attached to the chain-locker bulkhead or chain-locker divider, a tie rod or wire connecter should be installed between the diamond-eye plate and the keelson. A connecter

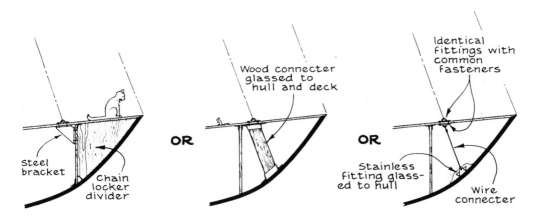

of solid wood might also be used. These installations are best done professionally to withstand the enormous strains involved. Fiberglassing to the hull or deck first requires grinding and cleaning, then laminating with epoxy resin.

If you own a large boat, consider removable-stay hardware that incorporates a quick-release Hyfield lever.

SLAP HAPPY

Hans Lankamp, who sails a Bayfield 25 called *Baydream* from Gloucester, Ontario, Canada, quieted his mast with plastic electrical-cable ties. He pulled the wires out of the base of the mast, having first attached retrieval messengers. As the wires were pulled out, he attached three cable ties in a 120-degree formation at intervals of 2 feet or so. He discovered that it is best to use large, stiff ties clipped to two-thirds of the mast's inside diameter. Once all the ties were attached to the mast wires, he pulled them back into the mast while flexing the plastic ties to aid entry. The halyards simply run up and down in the triangular spaces.

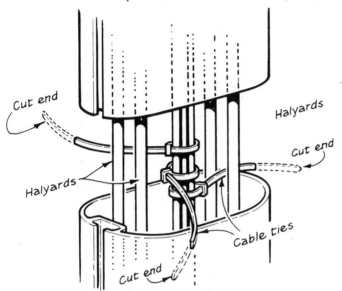

Bruno Caroit from Montreal attacked the mast-slap problem aboard his Asbury 33, *Tirelou*, by cutting plastic "spiders" out of empty gallon milk jugs and attaching them to the mast wires at intervals of 3 feet. To prevent the spiders from sliding downward, he seized the wires to the spiders with a little electrical tape. Notice in the sketch that the spiders are slightly larger than the mast section.

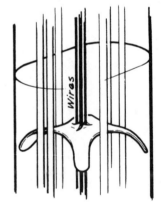

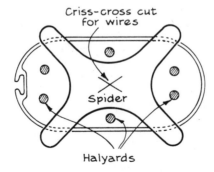

CHANGING HALYARDS AND OTHER KNOTTY PROBLEMS

If you've ever suffered the frustration of getting a new halyard mated to the old one to pass over a masthead sheave, you're sure to appreciate how William Harper solved this problem aboard

Harper's Ferry, a Gulfstar 47 from Clear Lake, Texas. Taping two halyards together results in a stiff joint that often comes apart high above the deck. But taping the old halyard to a small-diameter leader, then taping that to the new halyard has a far better chance of success. A better, more flexible, and much stronger method is simply to connect the old and new halyard ends together with a 6-inch length of heat-shrink tubing. The last technique also works beautifully when changing internal boom tackles.

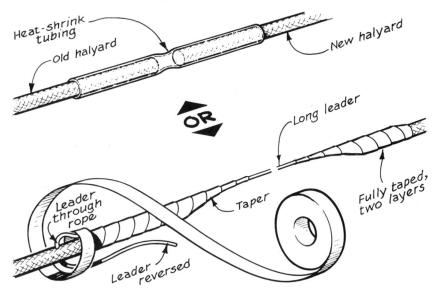

IN THE GROOVE

Ralph and Marion Thompstone, who sail a 35-foot Falmouth sloop named *Caper* from Bradenton, Florida, had been having trouble with sticking sail slides in the groove of the mast. Despite washing out salt and dirt, the slides would still hang up, especially when trying to douse canvas in a rising breeze. Then they made a lubricating slide out of lamp wick sewn around a strip of plastic.

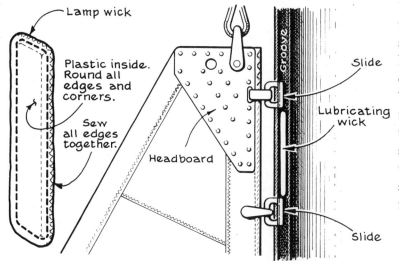

It's inserted between the two slides attached to the main headboard. Every couple of months, the Thompstones saturate the wick with their favorite silicone spray so every time they raise and lower sail, the extruded slot is lubricated.

BOBSTAY PROTECTION

On many boats with bowsprits, the bobstay fitting is very near or below the waterline when at rest. When underway, the bobstay fitting will be submerged almost all the time. So, electrolytic corrosion is always a danger to the fitting as well as the fastenings.

Stuart Miller, sailing *Quacker Jacque III*, a Hans Christian 33 out of Marblehead, Massachusetts, suggests that you make sure your bobstay fitting is bonded to your grounding system in the same way as all other major metal parts and equipment. For added protection, install a teardrop zinc anode at the bow of your boat, and connect it to the bobstay fitting with a bronze jumper strap (A).

During your next haulout, Stuart suggests that you check to see that other underwater fittings, such as rudder gudgeons, rudder-heel bearing, and stern-bearing housing, are electrolytically protected in the same way (B). Whenever possible, the jumper straps should be inside the hull and may be used to connect several hardware items to a single anode (C).

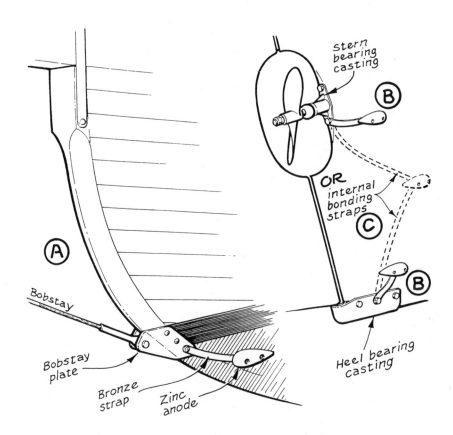

SECURING YOUR ENSIGN STAFF

Emil Gaynor from Camarillo, California, steered *Frenesi* through a quick jibe, came around, and retrieved the valuable staff and expensive nylon ensign that had blown out of the stern-rail socket. Had it been dark or the seas rough, chances are both would have been lost. The next day, Emil devised and fabricated a simple and inexpensive retaining pendant to help protect his colors from a watery fate. He suggests two possible methods of installing your own.

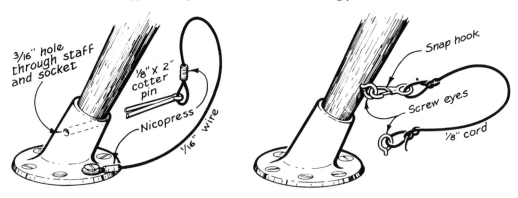

ROLLER-FURLING HEADSAIL EXTRUSION PROTECTION

To help prevent damaging the roller-furling headsail extrusion when removing the keel-stepped mast from his C&C 35, *Northern Loon*, Bud Morrison from Etobicoke, Ontario, Canada, attaches one end of a 4:1 self-cleating tackle to the eye under the lower swivel and the other end to the base of the mast. The tackle is fitted with a snap hook that slips onto the edge of the mast extrusion. The furler is pulled very tightly by the tackle while extra hands use towels to pad the mast at contact points. Once the mast is lowered to the horizontal position, the extrusion can be secured to the mast

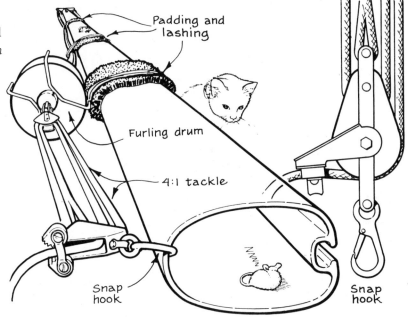

at close intervals or removed from the mast under complete control. By the way, the tackle that Bud uses is the boom vang removed from the mast and boom before unrigging the boat.

EXTENDING ENSIGN LIFE

Yacht ensigns are very expensive, but even the highest quality will fray and fade quickly if left flying at all times. The obvious solution is removal or covering when they are not in use, but convenience is the key to encouraging this practice.

John Brown, aboard *Gemini*, has made an ensign cover from foam pipe insulation that fastens to his backstay with ties. Protecting Old Glory is a simple matter of slipping the insulation over the ensign when it's not in use.

Another approach is to seize small rings to the backstay or install screw eyes on the ensign staff. Corresponding snap hooks are seized to the cringles of the ensign that allow quick attachment and removal.

Fabricating a light canvas sock that fits over the ensign and staff is a neat, yachtsmanlike solution that will assure longevity of your precious colors.

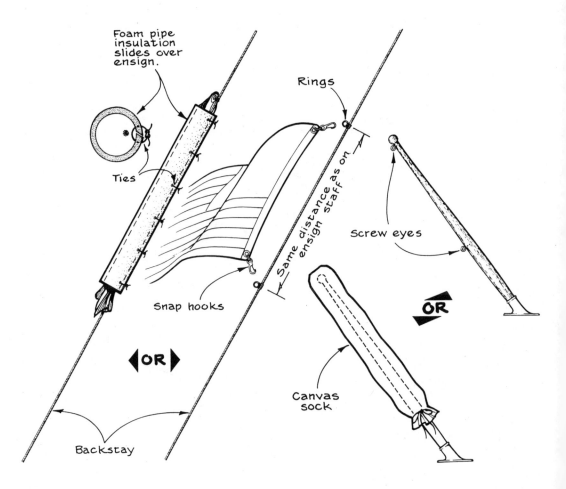

A NEW TWIST FOR AN OLD TRICK

You've probably seen the old trick that involves getting your opposing fingers stuck in a plaited, tubular device made from palm-frond strips. The harder you try to pull out your fingers, the more firmly they get stuck. Well, here are two variations on this theme for attaching leader lines for replacing halyards or internal-boom lines.

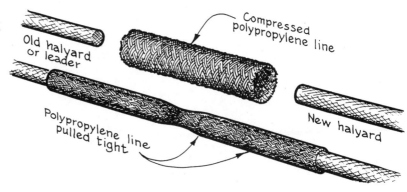

Dick Vale, who sails *Nike*, a Sabre 34, from Punta Gorda, Florida, suggests using a short length of hollow-braided polypropylene line to temporarily connect a large line to a small leader or another line. By pushing the ends of the polypropylene toward each other, the internal diameter will increase. Insert the line into one end and the leader into the other. A little tape around each end will assure the grip holds. When you pull on the line and the leader, the polypropylene will grip both.

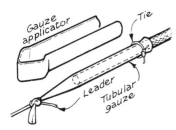

Kris Greene, who sails an O'Day 34 called *Mielle* from Annapolis, Maryland, takes the same approach. Instead of polypropylene, he uses tubular gauze, which is sold at any pharmacy as a finger dressing. To keep the gauze open and at largest possible diameter, he slips it onto a special applicator that comes with the gauze. Once the gauze has been slipped onto the line, the applicator is easily removed. Just tie the opposite end to the leader.

TREATMENT FOR SHOCK

Clifford Donley sails a Hunter 27 out of Toledo, Ohio, named *Celestra*. He was concerned about possible damage to blocks, fasteners, and cabintop caused by the excessive shock loads incurred when jibing in strong winds. Cliff found stainless compression springs made by Perko called "rope tighteners" and installed them between the blocks and the cabintop hardware. Larger compression springs

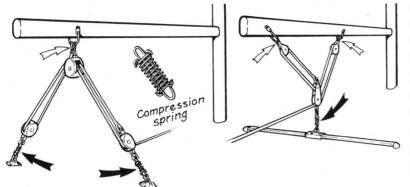

are available from aircraft-hardware suppliers or manufacturers listed in the *Thomas Register* at your library. The spring rating should match that of the smallest shackle in the system.

71

A HOMEMADE PIG STICK

Charles Chapin aboard *North Star* from Barrington, Rhode Island, likes to fly his flags. It's colorful, traditional, and very proper providing that each is in its rightful place. Wanting to show his club burgee from the main truck, he decided to make his own pig stick . . . a nonfouling swiveling staff for hoisting a flag clear of its halyard block and masthead. On ketches, yawls, and schooners, two pig sticks would be used for the club burgee and private signal, adding a very classy touch indeed.

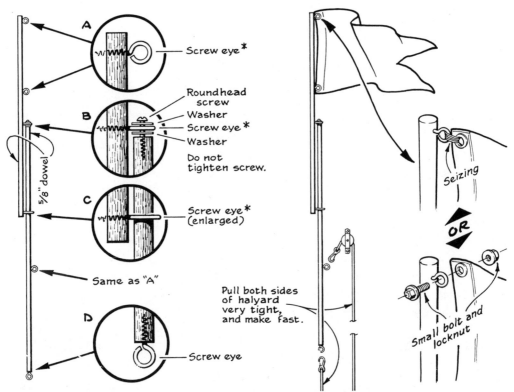

A — Screw eye *

Roundhead screw
Washer
B — Screw eye *
Washer
Do not tighten screw.

5/8" dowel

C — Screw eye * (enlarged)

Same as "A"

Pull both sides of halyard very tight, and make fast.

D — Screw eye

Seizing

OR

Small bolt and locknut

* Drill pilot holes for all screw eyes. File off screw eye points after installing.

HAUL AWAY

There are many occasions when manipulating heavy loads from the mast is desirable and advantageous: lifting a dinghy, hoisting heavy gear aboard, lowering large quantities of stores through a hatch, or lifting massive batteries for deposit dockside. If you have a foredeck windlass with a horizontal axis, you can often simply run a halyard directly to the capstan. But if your windlass is a vertical-axis type, you'll have a bit of a problem . . . in fact it won't work unless you do what Elizabeth Pearce has done aboard her Morgan 32, *Kokopeli*, from Seattle. She has installed several strategically placed heavy diamond eyes on the deck and cabintop that can receive snatch blocks. The block locations align the halyard with windlass drum so there is little chance of overriding turns.

When installing the diamond eyes, locate them as close as possible to well-secured bulkheads or other substantial structures. Use steel backing plates or plywood backing blocks to prevent concentrations of strain.

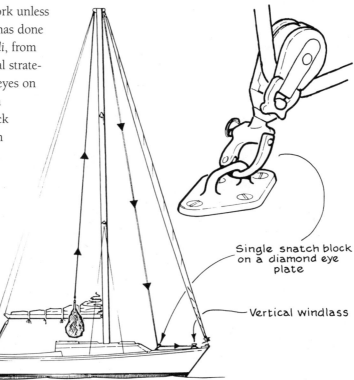

Single snatch block on a diamond eye plate

Vertical windlass

UP SHE GOES

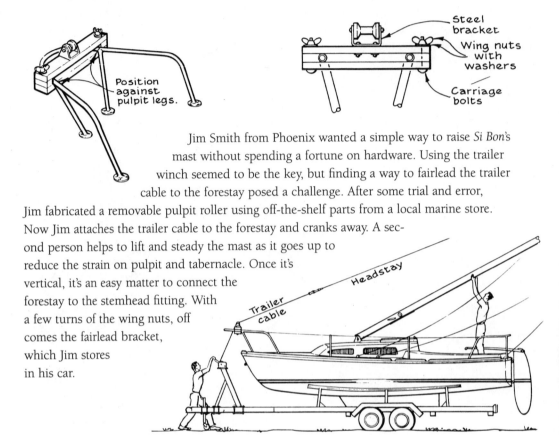

Steel
bracket

Wing nuts
with
washers

Carriage
bolts

Position
against
pulpit legs.

Jim Smith from Phoenix wanted a simple way to raise *Si Bon's* mast without spending a fortune on hardware. Using the trailer winch seemed to be the key, but finding a way to fairlead the trailer cable to the forestay posed a challenge. After some trial and error, Jim fabricated a removable pulpit roller using off-the-shelf parts from a local marine store. Now Jim attaches the trailer cable to the forestay and cranks away. A second person helps to lift and steady the mast as it goes up to reduce the strain on pulpit and tabernacle. Once it's vertical, it's an easy matter to connect the forestay to the stemhead fitting. With a few turns of the wing nuts, off comes the fairlead bracket, which Jim stores in his car.

Headstay

Trailer cable

CHAPTER 5

SALOON, GALLEY, AND HEAD

Every sailor devotes time and energy to making the spaces down below—the main saloon, the all-important galley, and the essential head—as comfortable and hardworking as possible. Luxuries, in the mind of the cruising sailor, are such things as the warmth of a cozy saloon on a stormy night or the ease of working in a well-equipped galley. Ideas here include many variations for a versatile saloon table, how to double the work surface in the galley, and squeezing a head into the tiniest space.

PINNIPED'S FOLDING TABLE

John Brand from Brisbane, California, created a saloon table aboard *Pinniped* that has impeccable logic and simplicity. It is well designed, easily constructed, strong, good looking, and effortlessly operated, and it instantly increases or decreases the table size by a factor of two. The tabletop is made up of two identical halves, piano-hinged together. The fixed-table half is supported by a permanent leg while the folding part receives a peg-fitted leg only when it's time to enlarge the table. Because the fiddles are removable, they can always be positioned on the "up" side of the tabletop, whichever it may be.

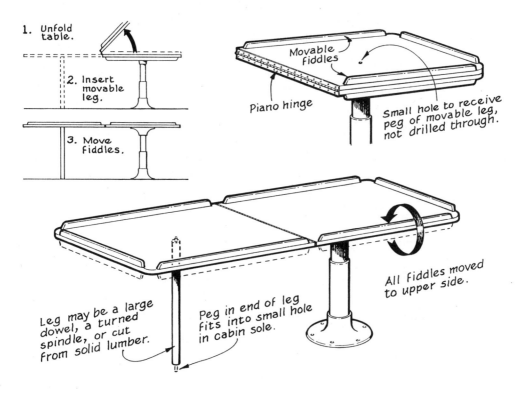

1. Unfold table.
2. Insert movable leg.
3. Move fiddles.

Movable fiddles

Piano hinge

Small hole to receive peg of movable leg, not drilled through.

Leg may be a large dowel, a turned spindle, or cut from solid lumber.

Peg in end of leg fits into small hole in cabin sole.

All fiddles moved to upper side.

MULTISERVICE TABLE

Every boatowner, designer, and builder knows that "multipurpose" or "multiservice" is often the key to efficient use of space or furnishings—for example, an awning used as a rain catcher or a settee also used as a berth. Well, Bob and Tanis Sales, from Bend, Oregon, deserve some kind of prize for the most multiuseful tabletop used aboard their Columbia 36, *Tolo Tsolo*.

The required berth-conversion insert for their saloon settee was also an ideal size for their dining table. This is not an uncommon multiuse technique. But their insert also works as a galley-range cover that provides vast expansion of the galley counter. What's more, by attaching special folding legs to the tabletop's underside, they found a convenient way to bridge the tiller in the cockpit for extensive topside dining. Using the same folding legs, the table is used to bridge the forward V-berth or cockpit to serve as an occasional workbench. Sometimes the table is even set up on the dock. Bob and Tanis have also been known to take their table ashore for picnics and beach barbecues.

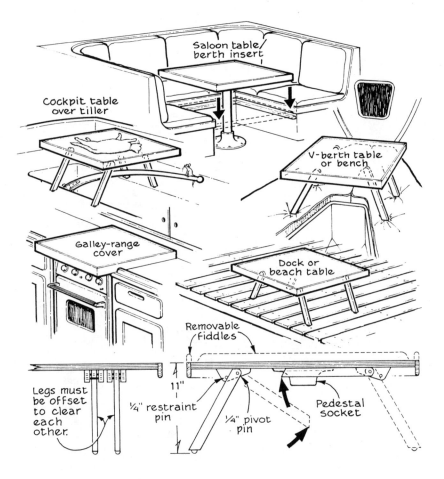

COMBINATION V-BERTH INSERT AND PORTABLE TABLE

Dee Widder, aboard *Tranquility* from Billerica, Massachusetts, uses the forward V-berth insert as a small, convenient table. This is done by simply installing three removable legs. Her conversion is fabricated from commonly available PVC pipe components (A), but hardwood leg kits with steel hardware can also be used for increased rigidity (B). The legs can be made to any desired length.

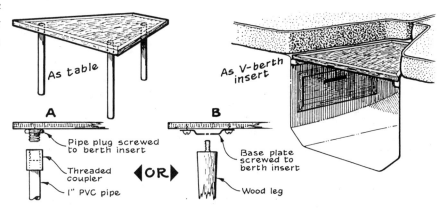

STIFFENING YOUR TABLE

Many saloon tables feel weak and flexible. You wouldn't dare sit on most of them! It's usually because the cabin sole or the tabletop is flexing in the area of the table-leg attachment.

    The best way to stiffen and strengthen your table is to reinforce both the sole and table. And the easiest way to do this is to install pieces of high-quality plywood to both surfaces. These should be glued and bolt- or screw-fastened. Finish the plywood to match the surrounding surfaces.

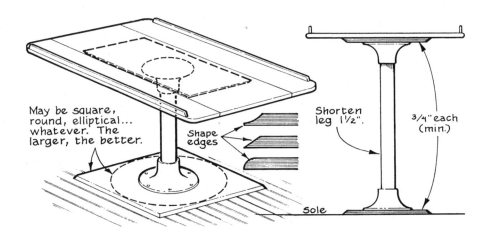

A Telescoping Tabletop

The saloon table aboard Donald Boone's sloop, *Itchy Feet*, was a very large, double-folding affair that was designed partly to fill the role as a portion of a double berth for guests. When in use, it gobbled up the available floor space. When stowed, the table covered most of the main bulkhead that could have been used for better purposes.

Then one day Donald cut the table into two parts! Now, that seems pretty drastic, but he did it in a way that allows him to reinstall the missing portion as an extension leaf. He found a set of new hardwood extension slides at a hardware store for about $25. He had considered dismantling an old extension table for about the same cost.

The forward parts of the table slides are fastened to the bulkhead, and the aft parts attached to the underside of the table. He was very careful to make sure that the slides are absolutely parallel and that the attachment screws don't interfere with the sliding action. Donald also installed a shock-cord restraint to prevent the table from detaching from the bulkhead.

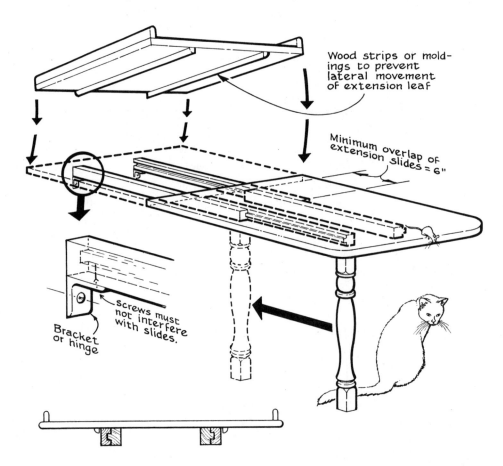

Wood strips or moldings to prevent lateral movement of extension leaf

Minimum overlap of extension slides = 6"

Screws must not interfere with slides.

Bracket or hinge

A TABLE/CABINET COMBO

Even aboard a Yorktown 39, efficient space usage is imperative, as Linda Davis from Seattle will tell you. Aboard *Pendragon*, almost every square foot is maximized, and "dual-function" is the norm rather than the exception. Take a look at the unusual saloon table that also serves as the door to a multipurpose cabinet.

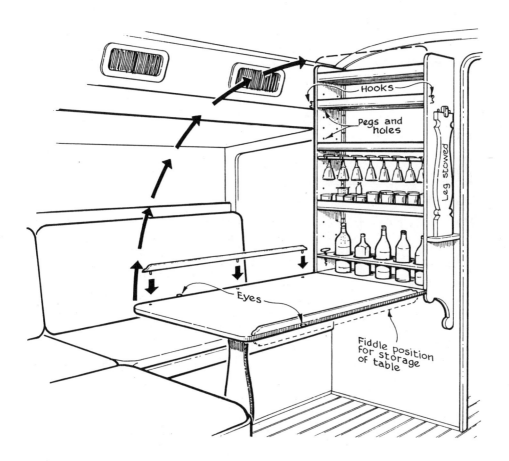

The cabinet was constructed using ½-inch marine plywood, veneered to match the ship's interior furniture and trim. Exposed edges were also covered with matching wood. The tabletop (aka, door) was constructed of 1-inch plywood to reduce twisting when in use. The cabinet was attached to the bulkhead with small wood cleats. Designed primarily to securely hold and show off *Pendragon*'s best crystal and glassware, several shelves are also adjustable using movable pegs as supports. The underside of the table (exposed side of the door) boasts a gorgeous marine print. The solid-wood table leg simply fits into holes in the table and the cabin sole. When not in use, the table leg is stowed on the cabinet side.

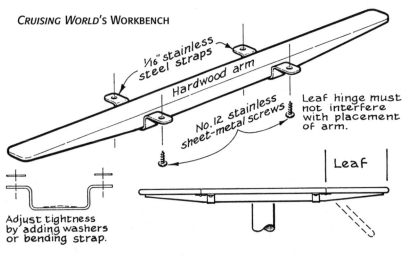

1/16" stainless steel straps

Hardwood arm

No.12 stainless sheet-metal screws

Leaf hinge must not interfere with placement of arm.

Leaf

Adjust tightness by adding washers or bending strap.

EXTENSION LEAVES

Extension leaves can add tremendously to the flexibility of your table arrangement as well as the use of your saloon space. Leaves when raised are normally supported by wood arms. For the leaves to be strong and rigid, the arms must be very stiff while easy to use. Arms that swivel on a single central bolt are usually floppy and become floppier with age and use. Inserting hardwood leaf arms through a pair of steel straps is one way of eliminating give when the extensions are in use.

SLIDE-AWAY SALOON TABLE

Once a saloon table is bolted down, fine-tuning its position is usually impossible. But John Herron, who sails a Mariner 38 sloop named *Freedom* out of Worton Creek, Maryland, wanted the flexibility to modify the saloon arrangement by moving the table at will without sacrificing security or safety. He consulted Lee Cherubini, the well-known boatbuilder in Delran, New Jersey, who devised and installed a unique table-mounting system. He attached a pair of modified genoa slide cars to each of the two table legs. Two of the stop buttons were removed while the others were left intact. Two lengths of genoa track were bolted to the saloon sole in troughs routed into the planking. Now, just by pulling the two slide-car buttons, the table can be moved and rigidly locked to any transverse position within a 3-foot range.

Lock button

Table leg

No. 12 or larger flat-head screw

Sole

Genoa-track car

Genoa track bolted to sole

Remove eye; drill and countersink for screws.

This system has worked so well that John believes it could be applied to mounting heavy topside gear such as LP tank boxes, storage chests, or a rigid dinghy.

SILKE'S SLIDING SALOON TABLE

Despite her 38-foot length, *Silke's* saloon always seemed congested. This was partly because of the permanently centered settee table. While cruising the South Pacific, John Aklonis thought that if he could modify the table so it could be moved or removed, it would open up his layout and provide some variety to the seating arrangement. Sure enough . . . he devised a system that allows him to move his table fore and aft, depending on the needs of the situation: aft during dining and forward most other times.

John also considered a design that would have accomplished the same results in which the table rotates on its leg. Interior space must be sufficient enough to allow the swiveling of the top. Notice in the sketch that the table leg is not centered under the table. This requires adequate reinforcement of the table and the sole.

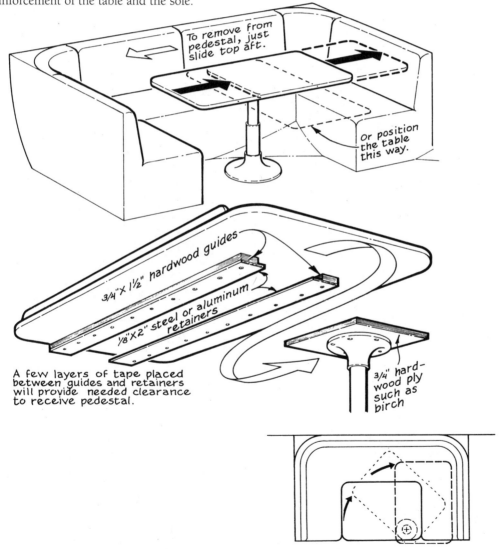

To remove from pedestal, just slide top aft.

Or position the table this way.

3/4" x 1½" hardwood guides

⅛" x 2" steel or aluminum retainers

A few layers of tape placed between guides and retainers will provide needed clearance to receive pedestal.

3/4" hardwood ply such as birch

PLEASE HAVE A SEAT

Brian and Cynthia O'Neill from Redwood City, California, thought it was time to replace the inadequate navigator's seat aboard their 1981 Cheoy Lee 44, *Akvavit*. Because metal-working skills would be required, they decided to have a professional fabricate the required parts out of stainless steel. The design that Brian drew was based on a commonly available swiveling secretary's chair with a hydraulic-lift mechanism. A screw-lift chair would have worked just as well. Only the chair with its attached vertical ram (or lift screw) was used in the final product. Cynthia gave the welder the chair's base because he thought he could put the casters to good use.

Most of the cantilevered seat design uses 2- by 1-inch stainless channel. The diameter of the vertical tube was chosen to just slip onto the seat's ram (or lift screw) without binding.

The hinge is made up of stainless rod and bent plate. The seat is removable by (1) pulling out the hinge rod or (2) lifting the seat out of the vertical tube. Keeping the seat in a fixed position when underway is simply a matter of adjusting the seat guys to suit.

The seat-bracket design may have to be modified slightly to fit your own needs. The cost to have the seat unit built will run about $200. Be sure that the seat is mounted with bolts to a very strong bulkhead or post that can support your cantilevered weight.

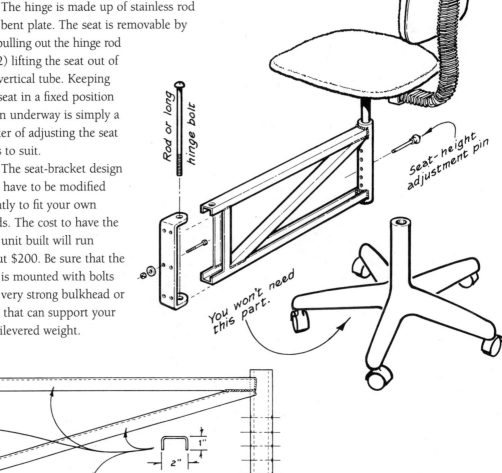

Rod or long hinge bolt

Seat-height adjustment pin

You won't need this part.

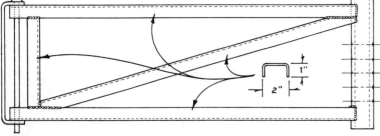

1"

2"

Dual-Purpose Work Surface

Extra galley work surface is always handy, and one that is gimbaled is invaluable. Bernie and June Francis gained both when they made a stovetop for the range aboard *Quest*. But wait! It's not just a work top . . . it's a giant-size plastic cutting board that they bought at a local discount store in Seattle. They simply made a cardboard pattern to fit the stove, transferred the shape to the plastic, cut the finished part with a hand jigsaw, then sanded the edges smooth. Voilà! Carrot sticks, anyone?

Groovy

When Tom Bradley and his wife, Jane, moved aboard *Promise*, their Pan Oceanic 43 from Port Orchard, Washington, there was not adequate storage for large carving or cooking knives. Using a table saw, Tom cut ½-inch-deep grooves into ¾-inch-thick lumber, taking care that the grooves lined up when the boards were glued together.

After sanding and varnishing, the new knife rack was hinged to a convenient galley bulkhead. A 7½-inch lid support was added to hold the rack at 45 degrees when in use. A small restraint cord also would have worked. When stowed, two small hooks hold the rack in the vertical position, and a couple of rubber pads screwed to the bulkhead prevent rattling.

Length of longest knife blade

Grooves (saw cuts) perfectly aligned

Glue sparingly

Lid support OR Restraint cord

Drop a bolt through the two screw eyes to lock the holder closed.

Small screw eyes

Small hinges

ALMOST INSTANT COUNTERTOP BINS

So, what do you do with the usually inaccessible space under a counter near the hull? Usually not much, but that waste of space was not acceptable to Richard and Dianne Hurst from Vancouver, Washington, who sail an O'Day 40 called *Stars*. They came up with the idea of carefully cutting squarish holes at appropriate locations and inserting Rubbermaid 1.6-quart canisters. Because the canisters have a slight taper, they won't fall through, are easily removed for cleaning, and can be covered for an almost flush installation. A permanent installation that prevents water from finding its way through the opening requires only a bead of caulk between the hole and the canister. The bins have proved to be excellent compartments for small galley items, personal toiletries, and even often-used tools and cockpit necessities.

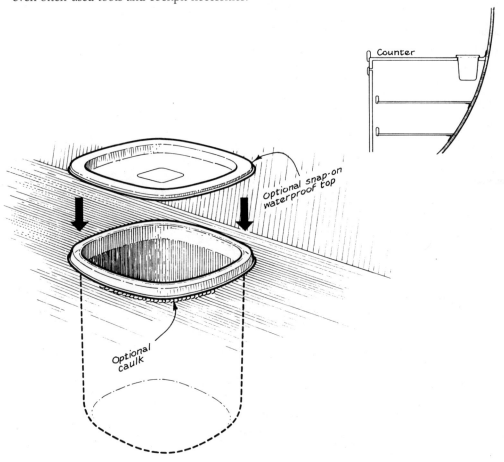

BEHIND-THE-LADDER TRASH OR RECYCLING BIN

The space behind the companionway ladder was not used very well aboard *Smooth Moves*, a Hughes 26 belonging to Paul Clegg from Waterloo, Ontario, Canada. In fact, for many years the space was kept clear to provide access to the engine compartment. Then Paul fabricated a lift-top box out of teak plywood fastened to the engine-compartment cover. The inside of the box holds two plastic swing-top litter containers with the tops discarded, manufactured by Tamor, which, in turn, receive plastic grocery bags. When needed, the lid of the bin

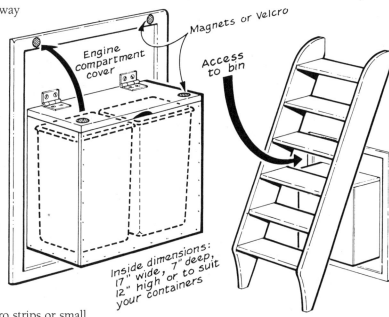

can be held open by pairs of Velcro strips or small magnets. The bin is positioned low enough to allow removal of the containers without moving the ladder, making bag changing very easy. Paul says that the bin has not impaired removal of the engine-compartment cover.

STAYING FRESH

You can prevent your spices from caking, aspirin from dissolving, and other moisture-sensitive contents from becoming stale when stored in bottles with screw-on tops. Bernie and June Francis, who sail *Quest* out of Seattle, suggest that you place a small packet of silica gel into each bottle. The packets, which can be dried periodically in a warm oven or on deck in the sun, are available from any electronics shop. Then, place an appropriately sized rubber O-ring into the bottle top. These cost only a few cents and can be found at your local hardware store. Silica gel can be harmful if ingested, so be sure the packet is free of tears or punctures.

A UNIQUE WATER-SAVING TECHNIQUE

Donna and Scott Hansen from Seattle have been using common spray bottles for all sorts of purposes aboard their J-36, *Bluejay*. How about saving lots of precious water by using spray bottles for a quick body cool-down on sweltering days, an alternative to sponge bathing, wetting and rinsing dishes when washing (the Hansens usually wash in seawater then rinse in fresh), rinsing toothbrushes, for hand washing, and cleaning the engine or other mechanical equipment. Donna says there are countless other practical ways of using mist instead of a solid stream under pressure. And Scott reminds us that spraying also saves an amazing amount of stored battery power.

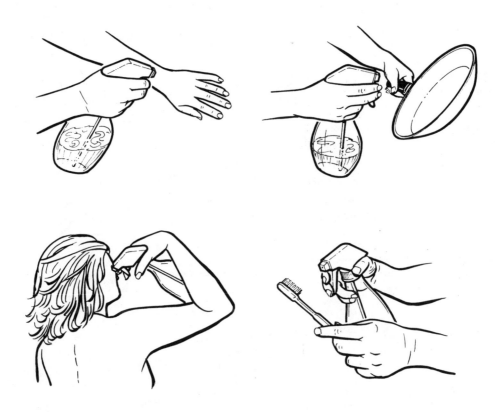

BABY, LIGHT MY FIRE!

Galley ovens are dark and mysterious places. In every oven there lives a gremlin dedicated to putting out matches or making sure they don't get near where they should for lighting the oven or broiler burners. The same gremlin makes sure your arm gets singed as punishment for infringing on its space. Peggy and Harold Erickson aboard the CT 41 ketch *Passages*, hailing from New York, beat the oven gremlin by making a great little brass stove-lighting match extender. They used a 2-inch electrical alligator clip, 5/32-inch brass tubing, and a small screw eye for hanging. The match is placed into the jaws of the clip before lighting. The same match extender is also the perfect barbecue grill lighter for the boat and home.

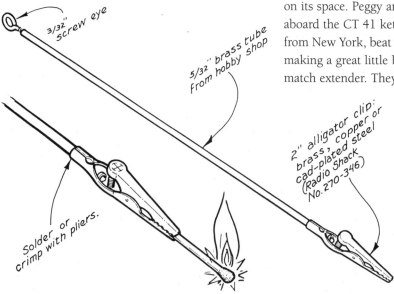

COOKING-UTENSIL OR TOOL HOLDER

Bulkheads and the backs of doors are inviting places to hang things on nails and small hooks. But hanging items always bang and rattle in a seaway and inevitably leave scratches on the wood surface. So Patricia Washburn and her son installed a Velcro storage system in the galley of *Lone Star* that solved these problems. It has worked so well that the same Velcro system is now used to stow the most commonly used small hand tools.

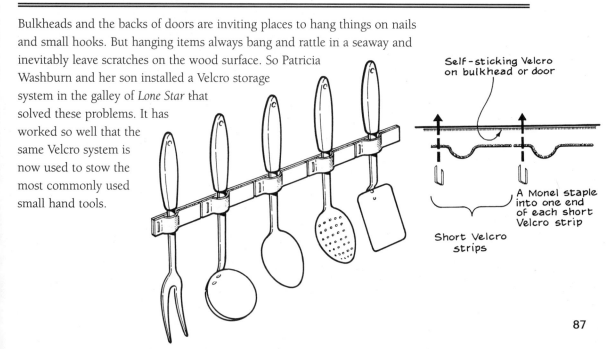

87

ADJUSTABLE, REMOVABLE, MODULAR ICEBOX BINS

Few boat manufacturers have tried to provide the "perfect" icebox configuration, knowing that every boatowner has a different idea of what it should be. Here are a few ideas for installing different types of modular units for convenience and flexibility suited to your own needs.

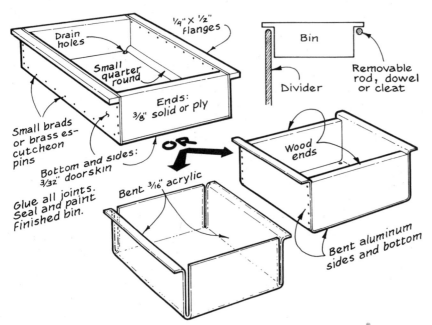

Gerald Crowley from Punta Gorda, Florida, installed removable vertical icebox dividers and horizontal cleats that support homemade wood trays. The trays vary in depth and can be positioned in several locations within the icebox.

Gerald's trays can also be fabricated of bent acrylic plastic or bent aluminum sheet attached to wood ends. You could also try inexpensive, commercially available stainless-steel food-service or baking pans or one of a variety of rectangular containers found at a local discount store.

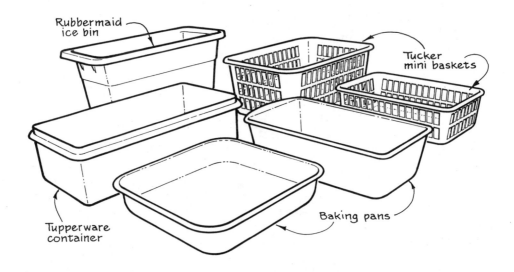

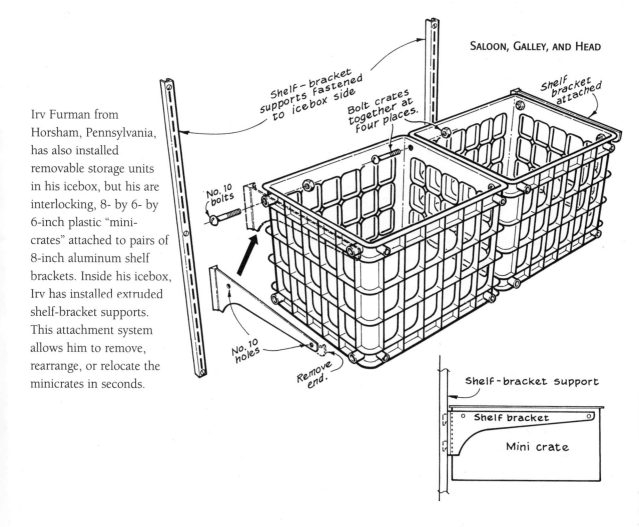

Irv Furman from Horsham, Pennsylvania, has also installed removable storage units in his icebox, but his are interlocking, 8- by 6- by 6-inch plastic "mini-crates" attached to pairs of 8-inch aluminum shelf brackets. Inside his icebox, Irv has installed extruded shelf-bracket supports. This attachment system allows him to remove, rearrange, or relocate the minicrates in seconds.

Shelf-bracket supports fastened to icebox side

Bolt crates together at four places.

Shelf bracket attached

No. 10 bolts

No. 10 holes

Remove end.

Shelf-bracket support

Shelf bracket

Mini crate

AN OLD NAVY TRICK

When rolling and pitching in heavy weather or when sailing to weather, keeping plates and utensils on the table might be a problem. But it's easily solved this way: dampen several paper towels, squeeze them dry, carefully unfold them and form them into a place mat. You'll find that almost anything will stay put, even on shiny surfaces under very extreme conditions. If you don't believe it, try it.

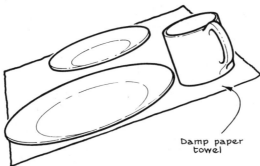

Damp paper towel

89

ICE-COLD WATER DISPENSER

Repeated icebox opening for removing cubes or chipping ice is a sure way of reducing cooling efficiency. Richard Poissant from Carignan, Québec, Canada, realized this when he took his homebuilt 25-footer to Florida and the Bahamas. To beat the problem, he installed a small hand pump in the top of his icebox and connected it to a common plastic jug kept inside. Connection from the jug to the pump is by way of ⅜-inch plastic tubing that is simply pushed into a hole drilled through the screw-on cap. A small hole is also needed for venting.

His cold-liquid dispenser works so well that he has installed a couple more; now he has one for water, one for iced tea, and another for fruit punch. The liquids come out so cold that he has almost eliminated the use of his precious ice cubes for cooling drinks.

If enough vertical space is not available, the pump can be mounted through the icebox front or routed through the icebox side and installed in an adjacent countertop.

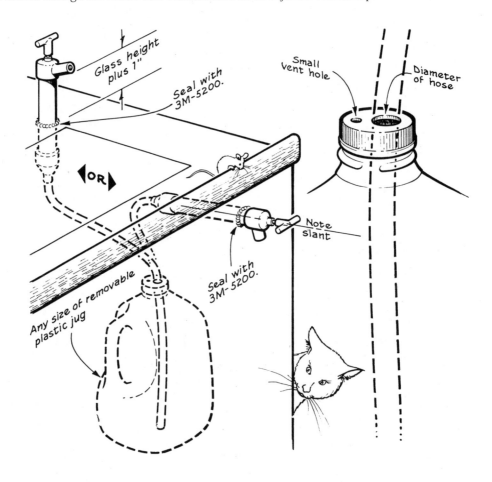

A REFRIGERATOR CURTAIN

Stuart Miller's 33-foot cutter, *Quacker Jacque III*, from Los Angeles, was built with two vertical doors on the front of the freezer and refrigerator. He could feel cold air pouring out whenever he

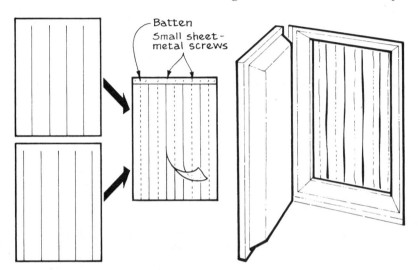

Batten
Small sheet-
metal screws

opened a door, and he knew that he had to increase efficiency. Then he saw a solution at the back of a frozen-food truck.

Stuart's fridge doors now sport flexible, two-layer plastic curtains. Slits in each layer are offset so the gaps on one layer are covered by the flaps in the other. He got the material from a commercial-refrigeration supplier. The savings in refrigerating energy have been remarkable.

NICE ICE

Vernon and Peggy Baumgardner live in the desert area of Rancho Mirage, California, over 100 miles from San Diego where they sail *Sea Quester*, their Catalina 30. Their boat has a great icebox but no mechanical refrigeration. So, do they buy ice? Oh no . . . they make their own. Each night before they drive to Mission Bay, they fill with water a plastic bladder that lines boxed wine, then place it in a freezer. By morning, it's solid as a rock and perfectly square. They leave the ice block in the cardboard box until they get to their boat. Once in the icebox, the bladder provides cold melted water through the built-in spigot.

COLD WATER, COLD WATER . . . GET YOUR COLD WATER HERE

Bruce and Ellie Murray sail the Brewer 42-foot ketch, *Encore*, out of Portsmouth, New Hampshire. It had everything they were looking for in a boat . . . everything, that is, except a source for really cold water. So the fridge top was open more often than practical just for getting ice cubes. The resulting detrimental effects on chilling efficiency were very apparent.

The Murrays' solution was to run a pressure water line to the fridge and connect it to a copper coil installed on the upper compartment wall. The high coil location prevented the water from freezing. In turn, the coil was connected to a spigot on the fridge top. Instant canned foam was applied for closure and insulation at the spigot and hose penetrations. Now they have ice-cold water any time the box is in operation.

Had the box not been mechanically chilled, but cooled with ice, the coil would have been located at the bottom of the compartment.

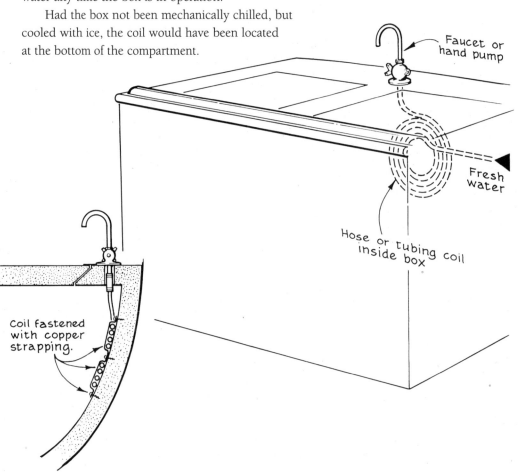

Faucet or hand pump

Fresh water

Hose or tubing coil inside box

Coil fastened with copper strapping.

WATER, WATER EVERYWHERE

Charles and Helga Althoff from Severna Park, Maryland, don't buy much ice. They freeze fresh water in recyclable gallon and half-gallon square plastic milk jugs and place them into the icebox aboard their Gulfstar 37, *Monopoly II*. As the ice melts, they drink the ice-cold water or use it for cooking. Water from thawing ice doesn't accumulate in the bottom of the box, so it doesn't become slimy and smelly. Some of the empty jugs are used to retain old engine oil.

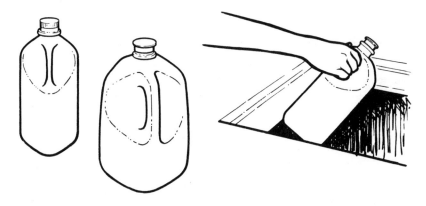

IT'S FREEZING IN HERE

Aboard *Florentine*, a Morgan 38 owned by Don and Florence Bottaro in Palm Beach, Florida, the freezer compartment (the aluminum evaporator unit) is very small. On long trips, there wasn't enough room to store both food and ice until Don made ice-tray hangers for the outer side of the freezer.

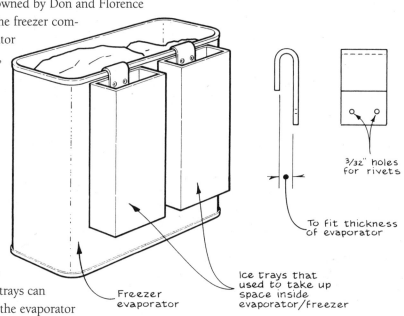

3/32" holes for rivets

To fit thickness of evaporator

Freezer evaporator

Ice trays that used to take up space inside evaporator/freezer

He cut a couple of 1- by 2-inch pieces out of ¹⁄₁₆-inch aluminum plate. He drilled two holes in each plate for ⅛-inch rivets, then bent over the upper third, leaving a gap of about ⅛ inch. Each plate was riveted to one of the ice trays. Now the ice trays can be hung on to the upper edge of the evaporator unit. This arrangement also allows for more trays to be used, and some may hold things like frozen vegetables and prefrozen ice cubes.

HOW COLD IS IT?

You probably don't know, unless yours is one of the very rare boats that was manufactured with icebox or freezer-temperature monitors as original equipment. A few degrees up or down can have a dramatic effect on how long milk, meats, or fruits and vegetables will last. You may also be wasting precious energy if your frozen-food compartment is hovering at 12°F when 21°F would assure freshness almost as well.

Bernie and June Francis from Seattle sure wanted to know before setting out on an extended cruise. June found a very inexpensive indoor-outdoor digital thermometer at a popular electronics store that runs on a three-year internal battery. It also has a 5-foot sensor wire that allows ample location alternatives. Bernie needed only to drill a ⅜-inch hole for the insertion of the sensor, which was later foam insulated. Installation took only 15 minutes. Their Tayana 37, *Quest*, now has digital readouts at the tops and bottoms of their chiller and freezer.

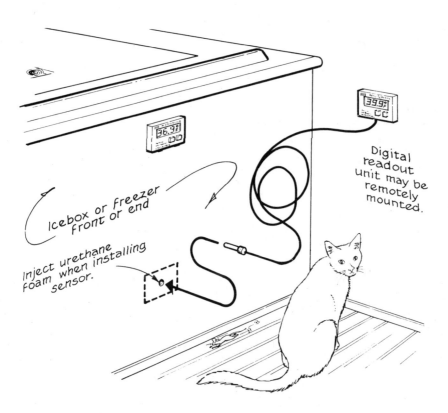

Icebox or freezer front or end

Inject urethane foam when installing sensor.

Digital readout unit may be remotely mounted.

PLEASE REMAIN SEATED

Cindy Grubbs and Dave Birkenmeyer from Ocala, Florida, have cruised the Caribbean aboard *Chrysalis*, a Pearson 365. During their passages, they have learned two offshore truths: (1) it's difficult to stay seated on the head while the boat is rolling, pitching, or heeling to an extreme; and (2) it might also be impossible to keep the seat from breaking or distorting its plastic hinges!

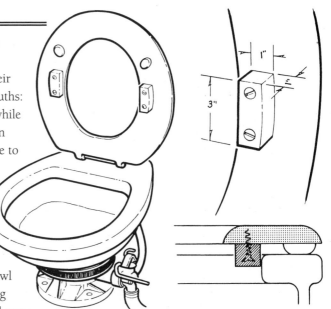

To solve the second problem, Dave and Cindy fabricated and installed 1- by 1- by 3-inch plastic retaining blocks to the underside of the toilet seat that just fit inside of the toilet bowl rim. Dave got his plastic from an old cutting board, but plastics shops will be able to sell you some scrap stock at very little cost.

A VERY COMPACT HEAD ARRANGEMENT

Harvey Lehman from Millersville, Pennsylvania, suggests an imaginative idea for designers and backyard builders looking for a way to install a complete head on a very small boat. This is simply the installation of a foldup sink vanity positioned directly over the toilet. When using the sink in the horizontal position, it drains directly into the toilet. To use the toilet, just raise the sink vanity, and secure it to the bulkheads with the barrel bolts.

Use of the sink is best restricted to relatively placid sailing conditions or while at anchor.

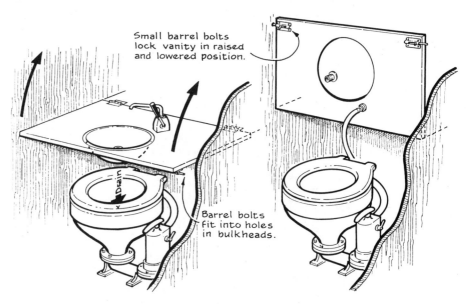

Small barrel bolts lock vanity in raised and lowered position.

Barrel bolts fit into holes in bulkheads.

Drain

ADDING SPACE

Most small boats suffer from compacted spaces that restrain personal movement and restrict foot space. This is particularly true in heads and forepeaks (A).

Bill Grabenstetter, from Rochester, New York, modified the standard door by installing a second one that operates like a bifold (B). It added several valuable square feet to his cramped head (C).

He suggests purchasing the new door from one of several marine-woodwork companies or a yacht builder to assure that it will hold up in the marine environment. The hooks and hinges should also be of marine quality.

This imaginative arrangement might have applications in other places on your boat.

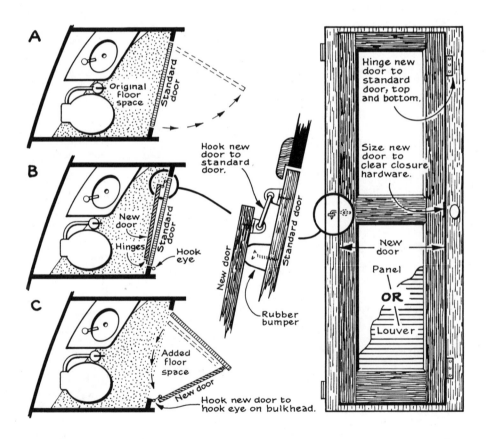

FITTED SHEETS

Making up a bunk using regular flat sheets is something akin to a wrestling match in a phone booth. Mary Richards from St. Marys, Georgia, is sure that custom-fitted sheets will add greatly to your life afloat, and she tells you how to make your own.

Spread out your fabric with the right side down. Place your mattress upside down on top of the fabric. Bring the fabric up and over the mattress on each side, then reach in and mark each corner from the inside using tailor's chalk. Measure and mark a cut line 2 inches inward from the bottom edges of the mattress for hems, then mark the material exactly where two adjacent edges meet.

Remove the sheet from the mattress. On the inside of the sheet, enhance your corner lines; these will become your sewing lines. Add ⅜ inch to these corners for cutting. Trim along the cut lines, and sew the hems as shown in the drawing. Finally, sew up all the corners from the inside of the sheet, rounding these seams liberally to prevent dog's ears. If you wish, you can add diagonals of elastic at each corner of the sheet for an extra snug fit.

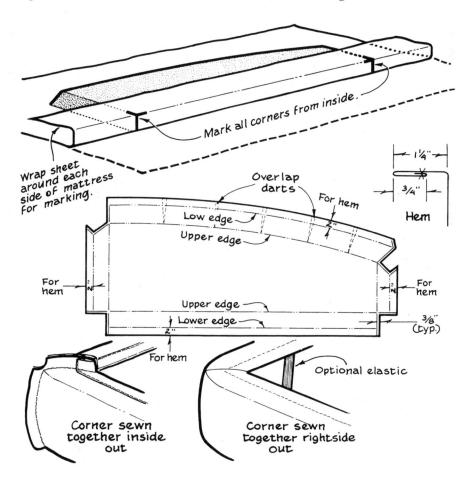

Mark all corners from inside.

Wrap sheet around each side of mattress for marking.

Overlap darts

For hem

Low edge

Upper edge

For hem

1¼"

¾"

Hem

For hem

Upper edge

Lower edge

2"

For hem

3/8" (typ.)

For hem

Optional elastic

Corner sewn together inside out

Corner sewn together rightside out

TRULY LUXURIOUS MATTRESSES

Pat and Bill England, aboard *Paradigm* from Ann Arbor, Michigan, wanted a lot more for a bed than a piece of foam on a plywood board. They checked prices for a custom-made spring mattress, but cost was prohibitive. Then they thought about modifying a futon mattress that can be cut to fit the berth shape. Most are made of combinations of foam and batting, could be washed or dry-cleaned, and are permanently fire retardant. They range from 4 to 9 inches thick, and begin at $200.

After careful measuring and opening one side of the mattress, they cut away the unneeded material using a very sharp butcher knife or a serrated bread knife. When they were sure it fit, they simply resewed the open edge.

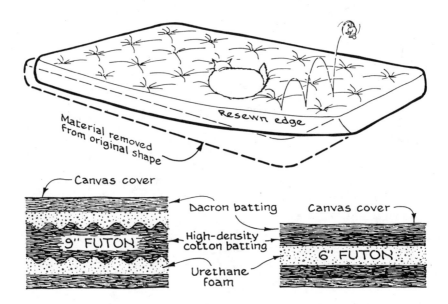

CHAPTER 6

COCKPIT

The moment a sailor lays hand on tiller or wheel, she is in command of the boat. She's also more or less stuck in the cockpit for a while, so turning command central into an efficient space makes sense. Whether it's a handy holder for the iced tea, a portable board for the chart, or a Bimini for shade, these ideas will keep a smile on the skipper's face

CARIBBEE'S QUICK AND CONVENIENT CLEAR CRIBBOARD

In the time it took to recite that troublesome tongue twister, Charlie Kemp could have buttoned up his beautiful boat and been back below! Huh? Here's how.

Instead of repeatedly installing and removing *Caribbee*'s rigid cribboard (hatchboards) every time a rain cloud passes, Charlie simply rolls up a 20-mil flexible clear polyurethane companionway closure and stows it on top of the hatch. This closure is not designed for heavy offshore weather, but it works great when dockside, at anchor, or when sailing in light stuff.

Charlie bought the polyurethane from a local sail loft. He cut it 4 inches wider than the companionway opening on each side. The upper edge of the closure is attached to the aft end of the hatch while the bottom edge is fitted with a pair of wood battens to provide weight. The entire installation cost less than $10.

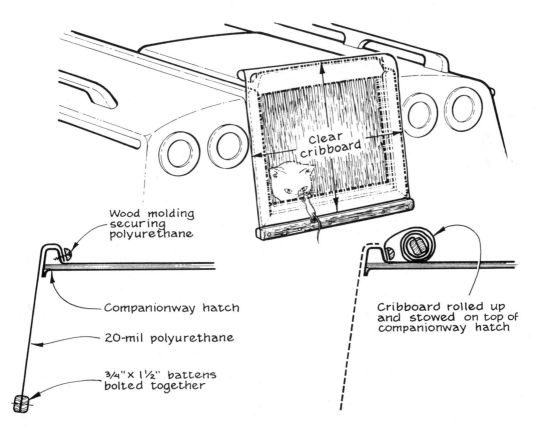

clear cribboard

Wood molding securing polyurethane

Companionway hatch

20-mil polyurethane

3/4" x 1½" battens bolted together

Cribboard rolled up and stowed on top of companionway hatch

SIDE SHADES FOR BIMINIS

Biminis would be great all the time if sunshine and rain fell only vertically. But in the high latitudes, and early and late in the day, a Bimini becomes less effective in keeping the sun out of the cockpit. Wind will also drive rain under the Bimini and possibly into an open companionway.

Arden Fowler, aboard *Second Encore* out of Cortez, Florida, devised a set of light canvas shades that can be easily fastened in a variety of positions below and around the Bimini top. By using bungee cord, hooks, and small rings, Arden's panels can be installed, moved, adjusted, or doused in seconds. Once the panels were in use, he discovered that he gained some control over the amount of wind passing through the cockpit. Additional privacy in crowded harbors was an unexpected bonus.

Small cord **OR** bungee with hook

Light canvas

SEAT-FRONT STORAGE RACK

To prevent his charts from blowing around and his guide books from getting in the way when not in use, Fred Hansen built an attractive and convenient teak rack that is attached to the cockpit-seat front. It worked so well that he made one for *Andante's* settee front down below.

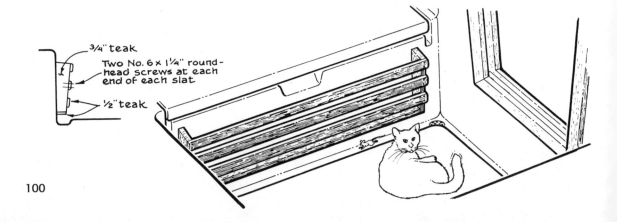

3/4" teak

Two No. 6 x 1¼" round-head screws at each end of each slat

½" teak

PORTABLE COCKPIT CHART BOARDS

Aboard Jack McKensie's *Sweet Marie* out of Cleveland, you'll find a ⅜-inch sheet of marine plywood covered with a sheet of 10-mil clear plastic that was purchased at an art supply store. The upper edge of the plastic is fastened to the ply with an aluminum or wood strip. The size of the board is restricted only by your storage space.

He can navigate directly on the chart with a lead pencil by simply lifting the plastic or on the plastic protector using a grease pencil or erasable marker.

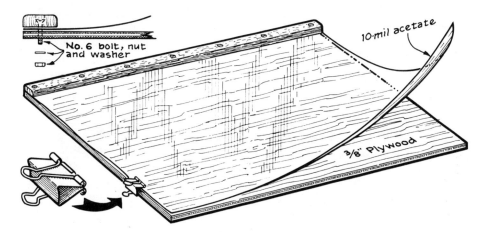

John Torrison, sailing aboard *Plover* from Alton, New Hampshire, has gone a step further by installing a hinged, rigid clear acrylic work top to his portable cockpit chart keeper. He has also added a nice looking and practical pencil rail.

As with the preceding chart board, size is restricted only by available flat storage space.

With either of these boards, charts can be attached directly on top of the board and plastic using the clamp-type binder clips available from office-supply stores. The chart boards may also be used below to increase the size of your navigation area.

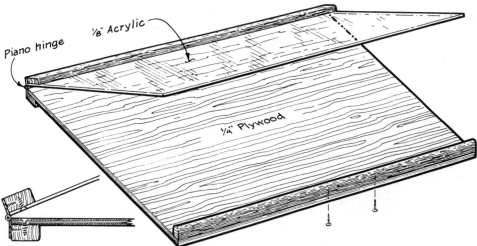

ENLARGED TABLE FOR WHEEL-STEERED BOATS

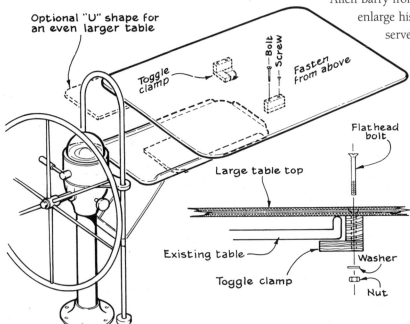

Optional "U" shape for an even larger table

Toggle clamp

Bolt

Screw

Fasten from above

Large table top

Flathead bolt

Existing table

Toggle clamp

Washer

Nut

Allen Barry from Milton, Massachusetts, wanted to enlarge his steering-pedestal table so he could serve meals in the cockpit of his sloop, *Second Wind*. The standard folding table was just too small.

Using ⅜-inch teak veneered plywood, he built a drop-on top that is secured with wood toggle clamps. He made it as large as his cockpit would accommodate, leaving enough room for adequate companionway access. Sizing your own tabletop is only a matter of choice and need.

If you're not handy, your pedestal manufacturer probably has extension-leaf tables available. Check its catalog for a variety of pedestal accessories.

A COMPANIONWAY SEAT

Aboard *Plover*, John Torrison's Sabre 28, you'll find a great little seat that fits onto one of the hatch cribboards. This allows John or his crew to sit fairly comfortably out of the weather under the dodger. It is particularly nice when alone in the cockpit while running under autopilot. His is made entirely of solid teak, but a good grade of marine plywood will do nicely. A custom-made cushion can be added easily.

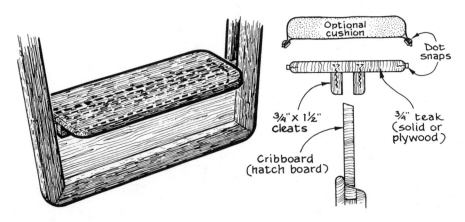

Optional cushion

Dot snaps

¾" x 1½" cleats

Cribboard (hatch board)

¾" teak (solid or plywood)

AN UNUSUAL AND VERSATILE COCKPIT ORGANIZER

Peter Summers from Largo, Florida, wanted a way of keeping things handy but not underfoot when at the helm. He needed an organizer that would accommodate combinations of items such as binoculars, a hand-bearing compass, flashlight, handheld VHF, and his thermal jug. *Querencia's* cockpit could not spare any space, so the organizer had to be compact when in use but instantly stowable.

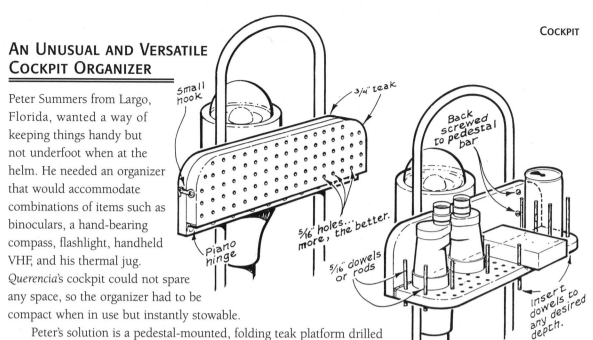

Peter's solution is a pedestal-mounted, folding teak platform drilled to receive movable dowels or rods that can be placed in a variety of positions as the circumstances require. When he is not using the organizer, Peter removes the dowels, raises the platform, and hooks it in its stowed position. After two years, nothing has fallen from the organizer, although rough seas have done their best to test it.

A COCKPIT TABLE FOR TILLER-STEERED BOATS

Carl Jensen solved the absence of a cockpit table aboard *Puffin* by building his own using teak plywood, 1-inch steel conduit, a couple of conduit straps, and a few scraps of wood. He rented a pipe bender for less than $10. The single leg is removable, and the double leg folds for easy storage. Removable fiddles can easily be added.

Paint the conduit to discourage rusting, or have the metal legs fabricated from ⅞-inch stainless tubing by a professional rail manufacturer.

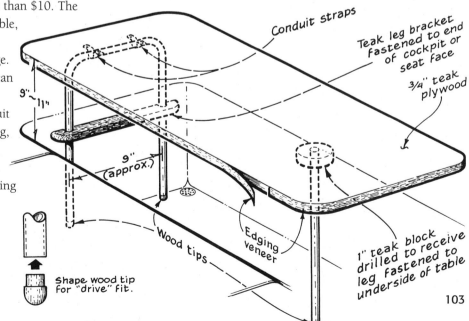

103

COCKPIT COMMUNICATOR

Battery-operated "chimer/pagers," available from several manufacturers, can be invaluable communication devices aboard boats. This is particularly true when the person at the helm is attempting to send signals to the foredeck amid the noise of engine, wind, and wave when anchoring. Awakening the oncoming watch, or calling for an extra hand from those below is another practical application of a chimer/pager. And imagine a lone helmsperson who falls overboard being able to send a cry for help to sleeping crew members with a chimer/pager.

These were exactly the thoughts of Ronald Vroom aboard *Outrageous* out of Hallock, Minnesota, when he saw a chimer/pager at a local RadioShack. He has since found other manufacturers, such as Maxtec in Van Nuys, California, that produce comparable products. Transmission range is about 100 feet, and the cost is about $20. The transmitter is only the size of a handheld calculator and can be kept operable in the wettest conditions by protecting it in a resealable plastic bag.

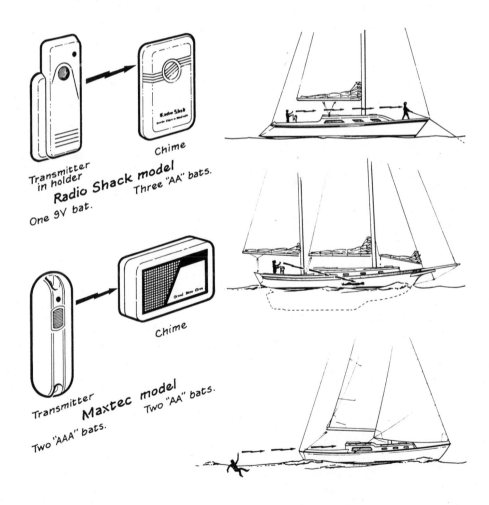

Chime

Transmitter in holder
Radio Shack model
Three "AA" bats.
One 9V bat.

Chime

Transmitter
Maxtec model
Two "AA" bats.
Two "AAA" bats.

A MULTIPURPOSE THERMOS HOLDER

It hangs on lifelines. It can be suspended from a counter or table fiddle. It can be hooked to the upper edge of a cabinet door. It can be slung from the front of a settee, and it can be laid on its side without rolling around. It's the thermos holder that Wade Carruth made for his Pacific Seacraft Dana, *Summer Girl*.

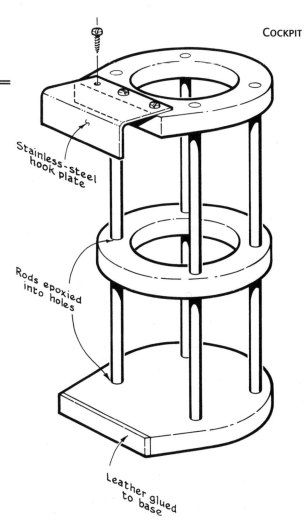

Stainless-steel hook plate

Rods epoxied into holes

Leather glued to base

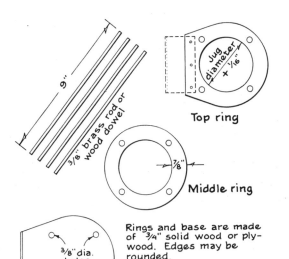

9"

3/8" brass rod or wood dowel

Jug diameter + 1/16"

Top ring

7/8"

Middle ring

3/8" dia. holes

Base

Rings and base are made of 3/4" solid wood or plywood. Edges may be rounded.

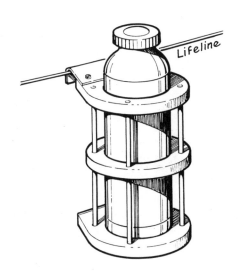

Lifeline

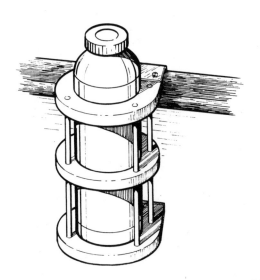

CHAPTER 7

DINGHIES

For the cruising sailor, a dinghy means access: to shore, to groceries, to a protected cove where the young ones can practice their tacks. So taking care of the little dink is a big deal. Our readers share their tips for everything from dinghy covers to sturdy painters.

A One-Sheet, One-Day Dory for Children

Donald M. Street Jr. is a marine writer who sails the well-known 91-year-old, 44-foot wood yawl *Iolaire*. In the mid-1980s, he developed and built a little dory for his son, Mark. Basic construction required only one sheet of plywood and a pleasant day's work (not counting finishing details). The completed product was a vessel with a sassy sheer and a friendly personality. You can build the same delightful dory with little more than a reciprocating saw, a hand drill, scissors, a sander, some small C-clamps, and a throwaway brush or two. Here's how.

Materials

- 1 4- by 8-foot sheet of ⅛-inch marine or aircraft birch plywood or Brunzeel marine mahogany for the highest quality; for considerably less cost but lower quality, you could use a lauan mahogany plywood "door skin"
- 40 feet of 2-inch 10-ounce fiberglass tape
- 1 quart of polyester or epoxy laminating resin
- 1 quart of cleaning solvent
- 1 small bag of microfiber from your fiberglass supplier
- 1 spool of 16-gauge steel wire
- 2 1-inch by 2-inch by 8-foot boards of clear fir, pine, spruce, or mahogany (for gunwale)
- waterproof glue; epoxy is best
- 1-inch by 8-inch by 4-foot clear pine, fir, spruce, or mahogany (for thwart, stern, oarlock brackets, transom reinforcement)
- 2 1½-inch-diameter pine closet poles (for oar shanks)
- 1 box of ½-inch copper tacks
- miscellaneous fasteners
- paint or varnish to suit
- 18 feet of fender material
- bow-painter eye, style to suit

Hull Construction

Lay out the sides, transom, breast hook, quarter knees, and oar blades on the plywood. Draw the half-pattern for the bottom on some wrapping paper. When you are satisfied with the curve, transfer the half-pattern to the plywood on one side of the bottom centerline. Turn the paper over, and draw the opposite side on the bottom. Cut all the pieces, and sand out irregularities.

Drill ¹/₁₆-inch holes at 4-inch intervals ⅛ inch from the edges of the chines, stem, and tran-

som corners of all ply-
wood pieces. It might be
best to temporarily tape
the dory together before
marking the hole posi-
tions to assure that they
line up properly.

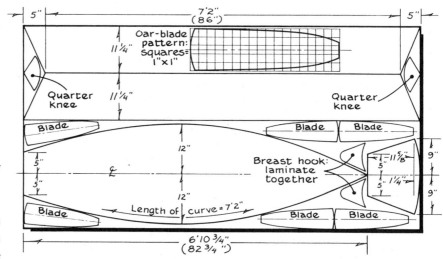

Cut 100 2-inch
lengths of wire. Now
"twist tie" the entire dory
together with the twists
on the outside.

Spread the gunwales
apart until the boat takes
on a pleasant flare (about
20 degrees) and a good-looking sheer. The bottom will develop rocker at the same time. When
you're satisfied with the look of the boat, insert a temporary scrap-wood spreader, and tape it
in position so it won't slip.

Mix a cupful of catalyzed resin and microfiber to the consistency of Spackle. Trowel a
smooth fillet of the microfiber mixture into all joints. Your thumb will work and so will a
teaspoon or tongue depressor. Additional cups of mixture will be necessary. Let the fillets cure
fully before proceeding.

Fiberglass-tape all joints on the inside of the dory. When the resin has cured, invert the dory.
Using pliers, pull out all the wire ties. Sand the edges to a fairly large radius (it's OK if you sand
right through the plywood), and fiberglass-tape the joints.

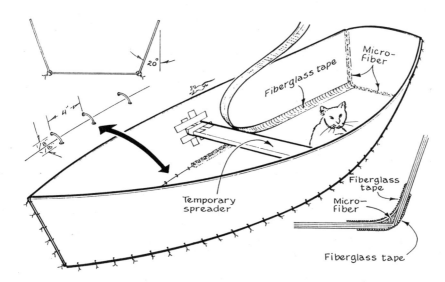

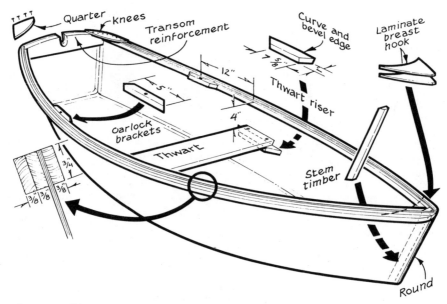

INTERIOR STRUCTURE

Cut the transom reinforcement, and fashion the stem timber. Using resin as a glue, fasten these parts by screwing from the outside of the hull. Sand the upper edges so they line up flush with the sheer. Cut a rounded slot into the upper edge of the transom for a sculling oar.

Rip (or have ripped) your 1-inch by 2-inch by 8-foot lumber so you end up with six 8-foot lengths of ¾- by ⅜-inch wood. Bend, glue, and clamp one length to the outside of each gunwale and screw fasten from the inside. If possible, do both sides simultaneously. Then prefit, bend, glue, clamp, and screw one strip to the inside of each gunwale, followed by the installation of the final strips to the outside.

Glue and copper tack the breast hook and the two quarter knees to the gunwales and the transom reinforcement. Sand the edges flush with the dory sides.

Now install the thwart. It's advisable to make a cardboard pattern, trimming it little by little until it fits correctly. Transfer the pattern to your lumber, beveling the ends to match the flare of the topsides. Round the forward and aft edges. While you're at it, cut a pair of matching thwart risers. Locate the thwart amidship, about 4 inches below the gunwale. Make sure it's parallel with the bottom, then mark the inside of the hull at the underside of the thwart. Glue and fasten the thwart risers to the inside of the hull, screwing from the outside. Now, screw the thwart to the risers.

Oarlock brackets are next. Fashion these as shown in the sketch, and break the exposed edges with sandpaper. Drill them for the correct oarlock shank diameter. Glue and screw these to the gunwales 12 inches aft of the aft edge of the seat.

EXTRAS

If the dory is to be dragged up beaches or over the edges of docks, you might want to add three bottom skids of ¾- by ¾-inch lumber. Bed them to the dory's bottom and screw fasten them from the inside.

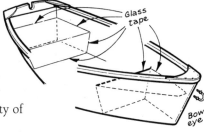

A skeg will also save wear and tear. More important, it will help the dory track straight when being rowed or towed. A skeg can be cut from ¾-inch lumber, well bedded and screw fastened from the inside.

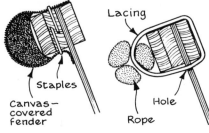

A gunwale fender can be as simple as a large-diameter rope laced with small stuff through holes under the gunwale. The best fender will be the commercially available canvas-covered foam, first stapled (use Monel staples) to the upper side of the gunwale, then to the underside.

Flotation is a must. With extra plywood and fiberglass tape, watertight compartments are added to the ends of the dory. These will add lots of strength and can serve as additional seats. Be sure to precoat the inside tank surfaces with resin before installation, and provide plugable drain holes.

An eye for a bow painter should be installed. Be sure it has plenty of backing, is bolt-fastened, and is reinforced with large flat washers.

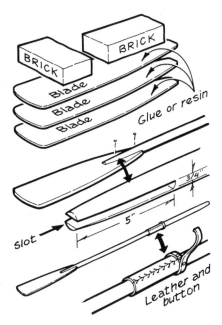

OARS

Cut the six oar-blade pieces. They can be laminated flat by coating the mating sides with glue or resin, then weighting them on a flat surface with bricks or other weights.

Cut a 5- by ¾-inch slot into the end of each oar shank, taper the shank ends as shown in the sketch, then glue and screw a blade into each. Sand the blade edges to a smooth round. Don't cut the final shank length until the oars have been painted and tried out. Add leathers and buttons to the oars' shanks to fit your oarlocks.

109

DINGHY STERN ROLLER

At one time or another, every sailor has had to row out an extra anchor, perhaps in anticipation of an approaching storm or just for extra security when leaving the boat for an extended period. And every sailor also learns how damaging anchor chain can be to a dinghy transom when the links are allowed to run unabated.

To solve this problem, John Brand, aboard *Pinniped*, a 35-foot Fantasia out of San Francisco, built a detachable anchor/chain roller, which can be used on either the hard dinghy or the inflatable. His roller bracket is made out of steel, but wood construction is also possible. The size and type of roller mostly hinges on the size of your anchor and chain and what is available. Check out the marine hardware catalogs and boat-trailer suppliers for options. Either way you build your roller bracket, be sure to install a chain-locking pin so your hands will be free for rowing or outboard operation.

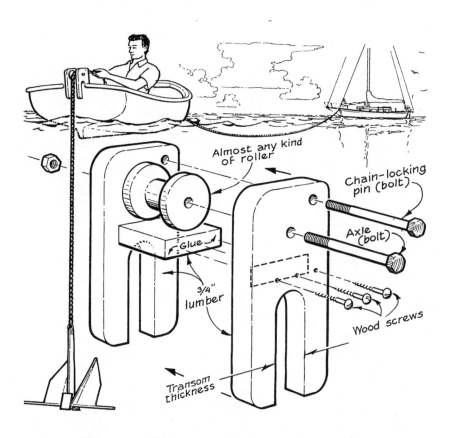

SAVING YOUR BACKSIDE

Emil Gaynor, from Camarillo, California, is very hard on his inflatable dinghy. When cruising on his Cal 46, *Frenesi*, he uses his dink for hauling anchor chain and all sorts of other abusive tasks that would have taken their toll on the transom. But Emil anticipated the potential damage and took measures to protect his trusty workhorse. He stripped and fiberglassed all accessible surfaces, added a sacrificial marine plywood motor pad, then installed stainless-steel half-oval molding to stave off chafe on vulnerable edges. After years of beating, the inflatable's transom is holding up great and shows promise of serving for many more.

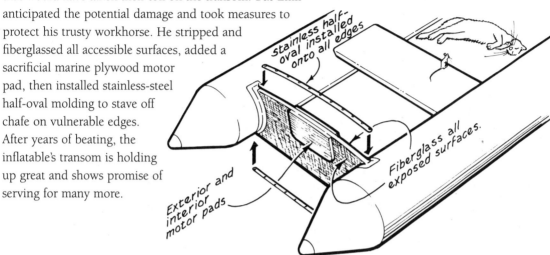

stainless half-oval installed onto all edges

Fiberglass all exposed surfaces.

Exterior and interior motor pads

SHOCK ABSORBERS

Michael Crane, who sails *Freight Train*, a Cape Dory 27 from Columbia, Missouri, offers an idea to help save wear and tear on dinghy gunwale fenders, especially if they're the expensive rope or canvas covered foam kind. Just purchase large-diameter foam pipe insulation (the kind with the slit along its length), and slip it over the entire gunwale and fender. The size will depend on your own dinghy. It will be hardly noticeable and will add tremendously to the chafe- and shock-absorbing ability of the dinghy's edge. It will also quiet the dinghy when tied alongside. If the dinghy is ever cabintop-stowed or carried on top of a car, the pipe insulation will provide valuable scratch protection. Replace as often as necessary.

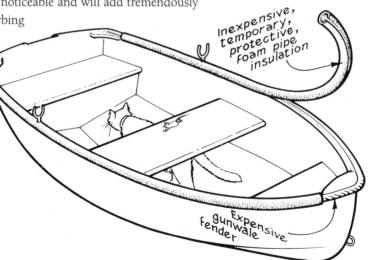

Inexpensive, temporary, protective, foam pipe insulation

Expensive gunwale fender

A NEW MEANING FOR THE TERM "SPRING LINE"

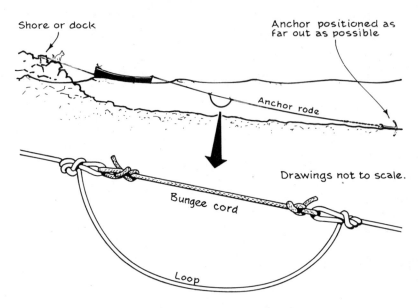

Shore or dock

Anchor positioned as far out as possible

Anchor rode

Drawings not to scale.

Bungee cord

Loop

Dinghies usually take a heck of a beating against docks or rocky shorelines, especially when it's choppy with an onshore wind. No one knows better than Chuck and Vicky Levday, who sail a 40-foot Lapworth sloop called *Contenta* from Sausalito, California.

They solved the problem by always using a stern kedge anchor that is dropped a considerable distance offshore as they work their way in. The rode is provided with a slack loop spanned by a 6-foot length of ½-inch bungee cord. Just before disembarking, they pull the stern rode fairly tight and make it fast. Then, they simply pay out the painter, and the bungee cord hauls the dinghy safely away from danger.

I ZINC THEY'RE BALANCED . . .

Pepper Sails lives on the Florida Sun Coast and cruises her Heritage West Indies 36, *Quest*, out of Pasadena, Florida. She didn't like the imbalance and wasted energy of pushing down the grip end of the 8-foot oars for her dinghy. Then she discovered that she could buy shaft zincs that fit the oar shanks. They cost from $12 to $17 and weigh between 3 and 5 pounds.

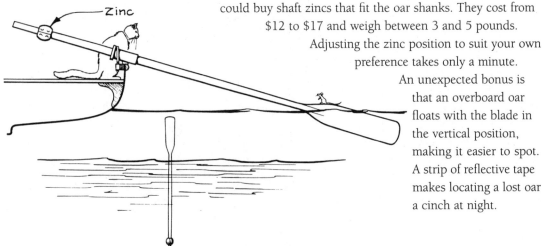

Zinc

Adjusting the zinc position to suit your own preference takes only a minute.

An unexpected bonus is that an overboard oar floats with the blade in the vertical position, making it easier to spot. A strip of reflective tape makes locating a lost oar a cinch at night.

OAR KEEPERS

What if you tow your dinghy a lot? What if it gets a bit rough or your dink has to deal with large powerboat wakes? What if you're afraid that your precious paddles will just disappear some night while you're asleep below? Will the oars stay in the boat? Larry Pompea, who sails *Fleetwing* out of Punta Gorda, Florida, deals with all the above on a daily basis. So he's come up with several ways of protecting his paddles that have worked perfectly for him. After ten years of dinghy towing, he hasn't lost a single oar.

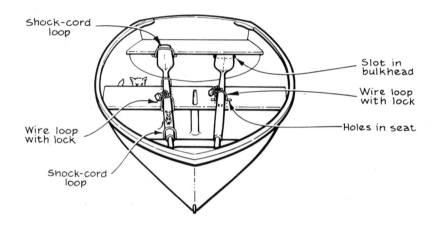

DUAL-PURPOSE OARS

Adding a boat hook to your dinghy's gear is as simple as attaching a modified brass clothing hook to the tip of an oar blade. Be sure you don't buy a brass-plated zinc casting, because it won't be very strong and won't survive in the marine environment.

Jay Johnson, who sails a 22-footer called *Gyp Sea X* on Lake Powell, Utah, added a hook to one of his oars by first cutting off the longer upper hook and filing the base smooth. He fastened the hook to the oar with brass bolts, washers, and nuts.

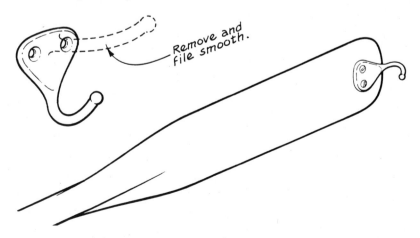

The use of a dodger is highly recommended when towing.

Eye bolts and large washers in transom

OR

Outboard bracket mount. Figure-eight knot

Upper painter

Lower painter

DO NOT TOW from single, center bow eye.

Towing bridles with snap hooks or snap shackles

Special towing eyes installed by your inflatable service station

Upper towing bridle

DOUBLE PAINTERS FOR INFLATABLES

Woodrow Lloyd, sailing *Petalu* out of Citrus Heights, California, often faces some pretty serious offshore towing of his inflatable. The manufacturer of his dinghy warns not to tow from the bow eye and recommends attaching the painter to a bridle fastened to opposing, forward, side eyes. Woody has a second upper pair of eyes installed as fairleads. His upper painter bridle passes through these fairleads to eye bolts in the dinghy's transom. He reports that he has had hundreds of trouble-free towing miles in very rough seas since installing this arrangement.

Installation of any hardware to your inflatable should only be done by a qualified, professional service center.

THE INS AND OUTS OF DINGHY INFLATION

For most sailors with inflatable dinghies, stowing the deflated boat in the smallest possible space—usually its storage valise—is a problem. Richard Gunzel from Darien, Connecticut, does it the easy way. He uses the suction side of a shop-style vacuum cleaner whose 1-inch hose fits the inlet and outlet valves of most inflatables. Then, before venturing on a cruise aboard his Pearson 28, *Genesis*, Richard reinflates the boat by using the exhaust outlet of the vacuum. Because many cruisers carry generators and AC-powered vacuums, this technique might apply equally well when underway.

SHSHSHSHSHSHSHSHSH.... (loud sucking sound)

ROUGH-DUTY DINGHY PAINTERS

Towing a dinghy offshore should be avoided whenever possible, especially if your boat has space for on-deck stowage. It can wreak havoc on your tender, lines, hardware, and nerves. But if you simply must tow offshore, or are towing your tender on a coastal cruise, these problems can be reduced by using "shock-loaded" twin painters secured at both ends to separate attachment points. The length of painters should be adjusted to take equal strains most of the time, which will dampen the dink's tendency to wander. Risk of painter failure is substantially less, and should dislodging of hardware or line chafe cause the loss of one, the remaining painter will assure that the dinghy will not be lost.

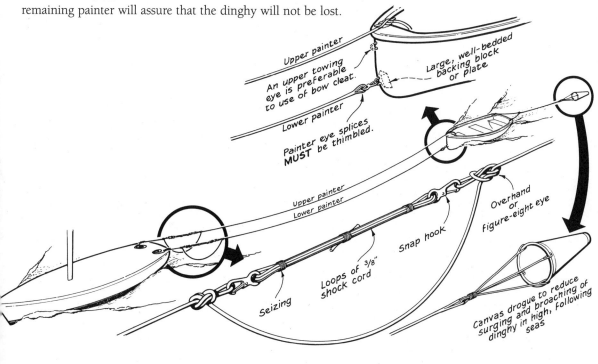

Upper painter

An upper towing eye is preferable to use of bow cleat.

Large, well-bedded backing block or plate

Lower painter

Painter eye splices MUST be thimbled.

Upper painter
Lower painter

Overhand or figure-eight eye

Snap hook

Loops of ⅜" shock cord

Seizing

Canvas drogue to reduce surging and broaching of dinghy in high, following seas

CONSIDER A DINGHY COVER

Your dinghy is one of your most valuable and used assets. A nice-looking and convenient cover will help keep it clean and dry. It will go a long way toward preserving your varnished seats and gunwale, as well as deterring theft of oars and other dinghy gear. A tight and secure cover is also an immeasurable plus offshore whether your dinghy is towed, stowed on deck, or triced up on davits.

Regardless of the type of cover you make, it's recommended that you wash the fabric several times before fitting and sewing up your cover to make sure that possible shrinkage has been allowed for.

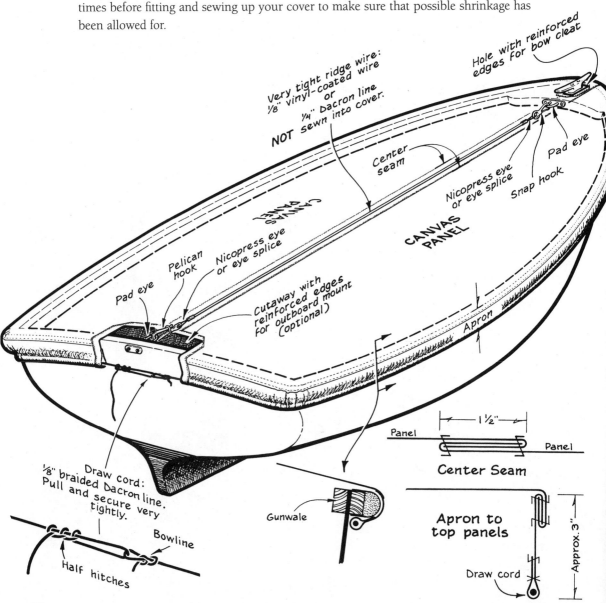

Very tight ridge wire: ⅛" vinyl-coated wire or ¼" Dacron line NOT sewn into cover.

Hole with reinforced edges for bow cleat

Center seam

CANVAS PANEL

Nicopress eye or eye splice

Pad eye

Snap hook

Pad eye

Pelican hook

Nicopress eye or eye splice

Cutaway with reinforced edges for outboard mount (optional)

Apron

Draw cord: ⅛" braided Dacron line. Pull and secure very tightly.

Bowline

Half hitches

Gunwale

Panel — 1½" — Panel

Center Seam

Apron to top panels

Draw cord

Approx. 3"

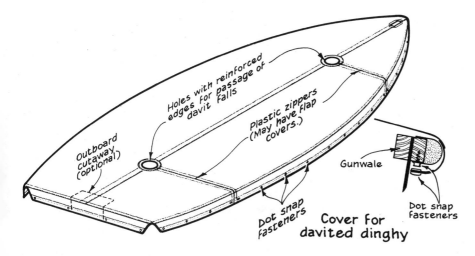

Cover for
davited dinghy

The construction for a davited dinghy cover requires zippered slits and openings for the passage of the davit falls. The openings should receive edging for appearance and chafe protection. Because a hemmed draw cord won't work with davits, it's best to use Dot snap fasteners installed under the gunwale and along the bottom edge of the apron piece.

Water-resistant canvas such as Sunbrella is excellent for dinghy covers, and it will be available in colors that match your ship's other covers.

DANGLING DINGHY

John McPeek from La Mesa, California, stows the inflatable dinghy on deck when underway aboard *Breezy*, his Cape Dory 25. But when moored or dockside, the small dinghy is stowed on a pair of hooks or chocks that rest on the upper rail of the pushpit.

The hooks are made of 1- by ⅝-inch steel bar that has been torch-bent following a pattern made by shaping a coat hanger to the proper configuration. After sandblasting, John metal primed the chocks, covered them with ½-inch foam, then spirally wrapped them with plastic tape.

John says his storage arrangement is almost as easy as davit storage, but a lot less expensive to install. And because the dinghy hangs vertically, he actually saves dockage fees.

Bent
steel bar

Pushpit

Foam padding

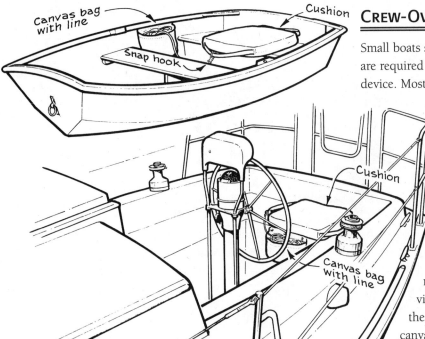

Canvas bag with line

Cushion

Snap hook

Cushion

Canvas bag with line

CREW-OVERBOARD CONNECTION

Small boats such as dinghies or daysailers are required to carry a throwable flotation device. Most often, this is a coast guard–approved flotation cushion. Most large boats also have a few of these cushions placed around the cockpit for passenger comfort.

Jim Smith from Phoenix, who sails *Si Bon*, an O'Day 192, has noticed that most throwable flotation devices do not have provisions for connecting ship to the overboard victim once he has gotten hold of the device. So Jim has installed a canvas bag to the side of his sloop, *Si Bon's* cockpit, as well as to the inside of the dinghy. Each bag contains over 100 feet of ³⁄₁₆-inch nylon line, flaked for easy deployment, that connects one of his cushions to the boat. In addition to aiding the retrieval of the person in the water, the cushion can be pulled in for another try if the first throw doesn't land close to the victim. Attaching the line to the cushion with a snap hook allows the cushion to be stowed when not in use.

STOP THAT DINGHY

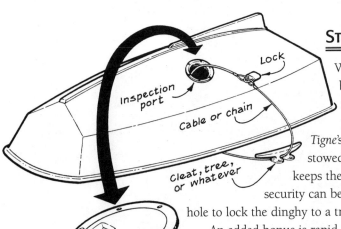

Lock

Inspection port

Cable or chain

Cleat, tree, or whatever

This part goes with you.

Who would steal a dinghy with a big hole in the bottom? The same question inspired Alan Lucas from Point Clare, Australia, to install a stock plastic inspection port in the bottom of *Renee Tigne's* tender. Whether the dinghy is beached, stowed on deck or davits, or resting on a dock, Alan keeps the inspection port cover in his pocket. Double security can be provided by passing a long cable through the hole to lock the dinghy to a tree or piling.

An added bonus is rapid drainage in the event of pooping when the dinghy is davit-stowed or when washing down the boat's interior. Another plus is seabottom-watching if you can find an inspection port with a clear cover.

DON'S DANDY DINGHY DOLLY

Don Hibbert Jr., sailing *Dream Time* out of Colchester, Connecticut, built a dinghy dolly using little more than a hacksaw, PVC pipe and couplings, a pair of off-the-shelf cart wheels, and some stainless rod. By not gluing some of the pieces, Don can remove them for easier storage. For an investment of less than $30, he's sure the dolly will provide many more years of service for his faithful tender.

PARTS AND MATERIALS

- 20 inches of ½-inch galvanized or stainless-steel rod
- 2 ½-inch cap nuts
- 1 (or 2) pair(s) of cart or lawn mower wheels from any hardware or home-improvement store
- 4 ¾-inch PVC elbows
- 4 ¾-inch PVC Ts
- 2 feet of ½-inch schedule 40 PVC pipe
- 2 feet of ¾-inch, thin-wall PVC pipe
- 4 feet of ¾-inch schedule 40 PVC pipe
- 1 small can of PVC cleaner
- 1 small can of PVC cement

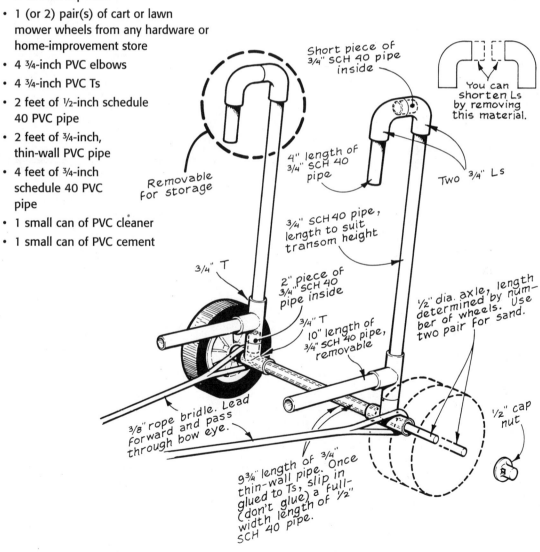

Bridle passed through bow eye

Dolly hooked over transom

Bridles knotted together

Short piece of ¾" SCH 40 pipe inside

You can shorten Ls by removing this material.

4" length of ¾" SCH 40 pipe

Two ¾" Ls

Removable for storage

¾" SCH 40 pipe, length to suit transom height

¾" T

2" piece of ¾" SCH 40 pipe inside

¾" T
10" length of ¾" SCH 40 pipe, removable

½" dia. axle, length determined by number of wheels. Use two pair for sand.

½" cap nut

3/8" rope bridle. Lead forward and pass through bow eye.

9¾" length of ¾" thin-wall pipe. Once glued to Ts, slip in (don't glue) a full-width length of ½" SCH 40 pipe.

119

NO MORE BLOWOUT

Ray Bishop sails around the Florida Keys aboard his 14-foot Peep Hen, *Chicklet*. It's impossible to stow a dinghy of any type, so he tows an inflatable everywhere he goes. Once, when inflating his dinghy, one of the chamber baffles blew out because of pressurized air on one side but none on the other. He learned a very expensive lesson. Now Ray protects the unseen baffles by simultaneous and even inflation of adjacent chambers. This is done simply by fitting a barbed plastic T into the pump hose and dividing the single line into two. If your inflatable has more than two chambers, just add more Ts and branch hoses so all chambers fill at the same time.

A DINGHY SPRAY SHIELD

Conbert Benneck from Glastonbury, Connecticut, just didn't like getting soaked when ferrying ashore in his dinghy from his Com-Pac 16, *Leppo*. Neither did his wife, Katrina, and she suggested in the strongest terms that he should find a way to reduce the spray. After a few sketches, Conbert thought he had the solution.

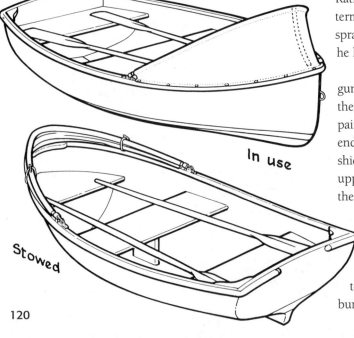

In use

Stowed

He bent ½-inch PVC pipe with a heat gun to conform to the bow of the dinghy, then attached the bow to the gunwale with a pair of small Bimini deck mounts and pipe ends. Using Sunbrella, he fabricated a spray shield to match *Leppo*'s canvas covers. The upper edge was sewn as a sleeve to fit onto the pipe while the bottom edge received Dot fasteners to hold it to the dinghy's gunwale. When in use, the spray shield is held up with a short batten sprung into position. When stowed, it is lowered to the gunwale and secured with small bungee cords.

CHAPTER 8

MACHINERY, PUMPS, AND OUTBOARDS

Systems supply a boat with many necessary safeguards. An auxiliary engine ensures that you won't drift windless for days or get pushed around in a strong current, and a bilge pump keeps the boat from sinking. Here, we get some nitty-gritty ideas from our fellow sailors: a peephole for keeping an eye on the often hard-to-reach engine, a manifold design for the pumps, and secure attachment points for the outboard.

PROTECTING THE PROTECTOR

When you install new zinc anodes to your shaft and hull, Wolfgang Scheuer from Fronreute, Germany, suggests that you dab a little bottom paint into the bolt holes and onto the immediate areas of the fastenings with a cotton swab. This will help to prevent the zincs from disintegrating prematurely at the fastenings, which could cause the protectors to fall off.

When installing a new shaft zinc, sand the shaft to bright metal in the area of the anode to assure a good contact between the shaft and the zinc.

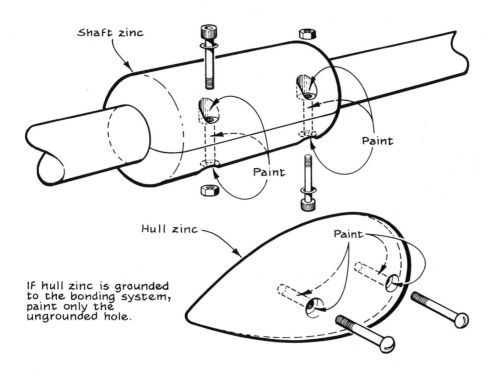

Shaft zinc

Paint

Paint

Hull zinc

Paint

If hull zinc is grounded to the bonding system, paint only the ungrounded hole.

WATCHING YOUR ENGINE

Bill and Pat England, from Ann Arbor, Michigan, sail around on *Paradigm* and know how important it is to stay in touch with the engine room, especially when underway. Not to look in now and then is to court disaster. An occasional glance can reveal a leaking stuffing box, smoke, evidence of unexpected oil, loose engine parts, chafing hoses, or numerous other mechanical maladies. To make observation more convenient, the Englands built a replaceable compartment closure using two layers of Lexan with a small air space between to insulate sound and heat. On one compartment side, they installed a double-layer Lexan port. To illuminate the compartment, an outside light switch has been located in an easily accessible position.

When the Englands are just out for a short day sail, or snuggled down at the dock, the standard wood compartment closure is put in place. It has been fitted with a wide-angle door peephole so they can easily look in now and then.

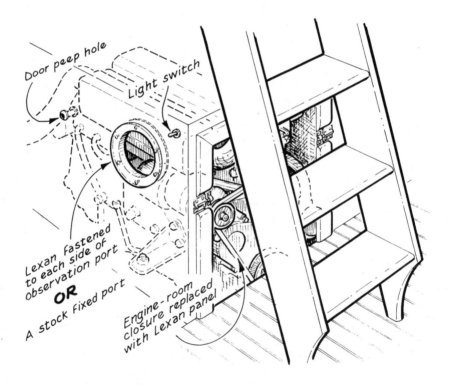

Door peep hole

Light switch

Lexan fastened to each side of observation port **OR** A stock fixed port

Engine-room closure replaced with Lexan panel

ADDING ENGINE-ROOM VISIBILITY

Unless you have a very large boat with a cavernous engine space or an engine room with several ample openings, you undoubtedly have a problem seeing all sides of the engine, transmission, and other equipment. You can solve this problem in the same way that Dave Rosenberger from St. Petersburg, Florida, did aboard *Zephyrus*. He installed several mirrors strategically placed on various engine-room bulkheads.

Glass mirrors can be used if properly secured, but break-resistant mirror material can be purchased at any plastic supplier. It can be sawed and drilled like most other sheet plastics. Car rearview and side mirrors can readily be found at all auto-accessory stores.

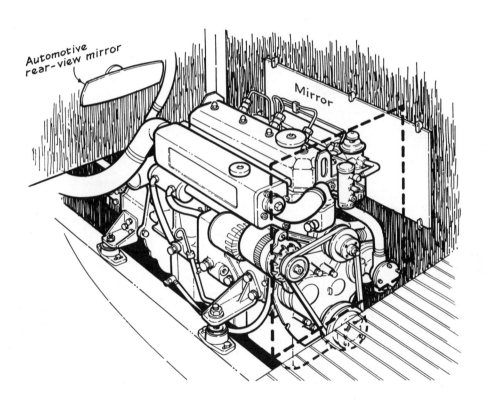

POP GOES THE IMPELLER

Bending and getting all 6, 8, or 10 impeller blades to pop into a water-pump chamber is a little bit like balancing a bunch of plates on the ends of sticks. Why not try a method devised by Dave Nofs, aboard *Fia* from Holmes Beach, Florida? (1) Place a hose clamp around the impeller and tighten it until the blades just begin to bend. (2) Rotate the hose clamp to cause the blades to flex in the correct direction. (3) Then continue tightening the hose clamp until the impeller radius is decidedly smaller than the pump chamber. (4) Place the clamped impeller directly over the chamber opening. (5) Finally, push the impeller through the hose clamp with your thumbs. It will pop right into the chamber with no effort.

A KEEP-CLEAN PROP METHOD

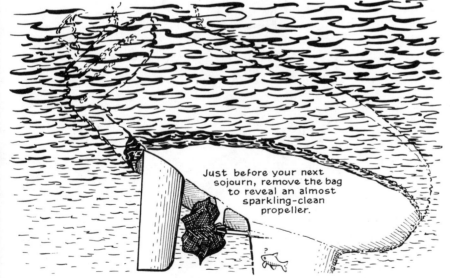

Just before your next sojourn, remove the bag to reveal an almost sparkling-clean propeller.

No matter how extensively you cruise, there may be times when your boat will be docked or moored for weeks, maybe even months. And nothing is more conducive to prop fouling than lack of use.

Steve and Donna Hamber aboard *Kaiolohia* have successfully implemented an amazingly simple procedure that you might try during your next long layover.

Drop over the side and slip a black plastic garbage bag over the prop. Tie the open end of the bag to the shaft with any small twine using a bow knot for easy underwater removal. Very little can grow in the resulting pitch-black environment.

OPERATING UNDER TENSION

No hammers, no long screwdrivers, no lengths of pipe, no large wrenches . . . just an inexpensive galvanized steel or aluminum turnbuckle will do the trick . . . tightening your engine V-belts, that is. Richard Carleton, aboard his Caliber 38, *Smiles*, out of Barrington, Rhode Island, explains.

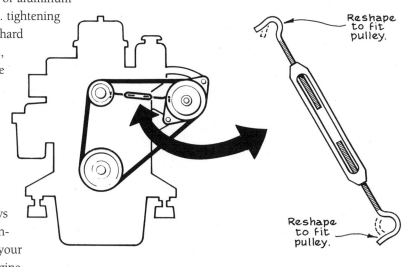

Modify a hook-and-hook turnbuckle slightly by bending the hooks so they nest in the opposing pulley grooves. Once positioned, just screw the turnbuckle body so the turnbuckle lengthens. As it does, the pulleys are pushed farther apart, tightening the belt. Don't overtension your belts. Be sure to follow your engine manufacturer's specifications.

A LIFE AND BOAT SAVER

William Dunlop from Thunder Bay, Ontario, Canada, was sailing his Tanzer 22, *Windrose*, when he heard a call for help from a nearby sinking boat. He helped bail by bucket for hours until the Coast Guard arrived. After the incident, William realized that he would have been more help if he'd had a powerful portable pump. He also thought that such a pump might bail his own boat out of trouble someday. So he bought a 2,000 gph, 12-volt submersible pump (a nonsubmersible pump with a long hose mounted to a board also would have worked) and fitted it

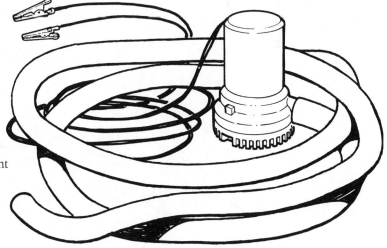

with 30 feet of 12-gauge wire with an in-line switch. Alligator clips were added so the pump could be connected to battery posts aboard his own or another's boat.

SHAFT SECURITY

Packing gland

Collar

Half flange

Your boat's propeller shaft is secured by set screws in the neck of the half-shaft flange. It is vitally important that these set screws be correctly and tightly seated in their corresponding shaft detents. To prevent the set screws from loosening, you should apply a thread-lock fluid. Finally, safety wiring the set screws with Monel or stainless wire is an absolute must. Periodic inspection and retightening and rewiring of these set screws should be a part of your normal maintenance routine.

Failure of the set screws can lead to disastrous results in some boats. When the boat is put in reverse, the shaft and propeller can back partially out of the boat or can even be lost. The sickening sound of gushing seawater through the empty packing gland (stuffing box) and the total lack of ship's propulsion can become life-threatening. You can prevent such a shaft back-out by attaching a shaft retaining collar to the shaft just forward of the packing gland. Jay Santos from Yerington, Nevada, uses a shaft zinc to accomplish the same result at far less cost.

Safety wire

Engine half flange

Shaft half flange

Set screw each side

Shaft stops when prop hits rudder.

Gear box

Partial shaft pull out

Complete shaft pull out

Shaft-retaining collar

Shaft zinc used as retaining collar

CAUGHT IN THE NET

Some bilge strainers use a perforated metal strainer while others employ a screen insert. Either way, when they corrode and deteriorate, you may not easily find a replacement.

Peter Keen, who sails *White Winds*, a Hylas 44, out of Boston, suggests you simply cut an appropriately sized square of nylon screen, form it around the strainer head, and secure it with a couple of plastic cable ties. You can also do the same thing for hand bilge pumps and hose siphons.

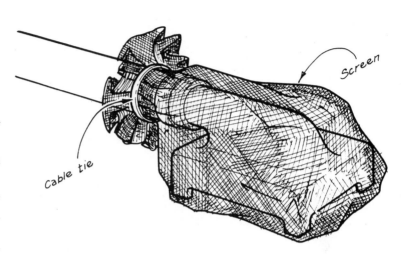

UH-OH ... WHERE DID IT GO?

Your engine began to overheat, so you replaced the raw-water pump impeller that had lost several of its blades. Upon restarting the engine, the overheating problem persisted. Probably, the missing impeller blades and rubber fragments had been pushed downstream until they became lodged at hose connections or pipe elbows or in the heat-exchanger plenum, thus causing a water shutdown or reduced flow.

To solve the problem of impeller pieces and other things choking your raw-water cooling system, simply install an in-line water strainer as close as possible to the pressure (outlet) side of the water pump.

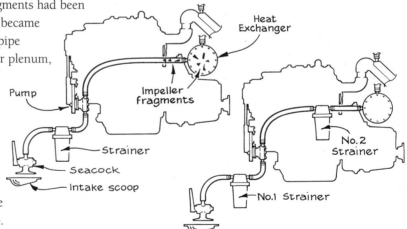

A FUEL QUALITY MONITOR

When Hazel and Murray Switzer from Brampton, Ontario, Canada, cruised the length of the East Coast aboard their boat, *H.M.S. Destiny*, their engine ingested some contaminated fuel. Although the delay and mechanical damage was minimal, it could have been a very serious matter. To help prevent a future occurrence of foul fuel, the Switzers fabricated their own simple and inexpensive fuel monitor and tank cleaner. They bought all the parts and materials at the same marine store for less than $12. Once a month, they insert the copper tube through the inspection plate, and place its end at the lowest part of the tank. The monitor's outlet hose is placed into a large glass jar (restaurants are a source for 1-gallon pickle jars). About two hours after pumping fuel into the jar, water and solid contaminates have settled to the bottom and will be visible. To clean the tank, this process is repeated until the fuel is perfectly clear. To avoid fuel mess and odor, Murray stores the fuel-monitor parts in a sealed plastic bag.

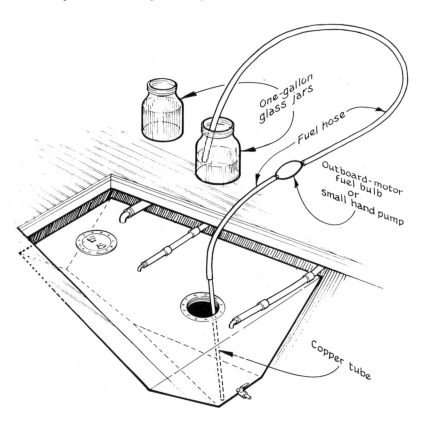

COOL IT

Every quarter and before extended cruises, you should inspect your engine's cooling system. All worn, broken, or questionable parts should be replaced. Here's a list of things to check. (1) Are all hoses free of cracks or chafe? (2) Are hose clamps tight and rust-free? (3) Is there any sign of play in the water-pump bearings? (4) Is there any debris in the raw-water side of the heat exchanger? (5) Are the engine-block and heat-exchanger zincs in good shape? (6) How do the V-belts look? (7) Are the belt tensions correct? (8) What's the condition of the raw-water impeller? (9) Does the freshwater system need flushing? (10) Is the water/coolant ratio correct? (11) Is the thermostat accurate? (12) Is the intake scoop, seacock, and strainer clear? (13) How's the freshwater level? Everything OK? Then let's go!

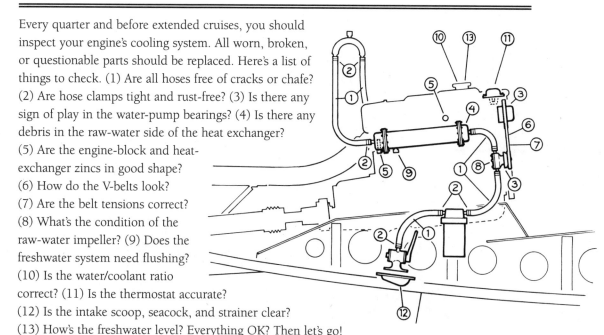

GOOD FOR THE LAST DROP

If you drain your engine oil by sticking an oil-resistant hose through the oil-level dipstick opening, the chances are that the tube bends inside the sump and is unable to reach all the old oil. Paul Geil, who sails *Silk Stone*, a C&C 35 out of Ludington, Michigan, suggests that you attach your oil suction hose to a short length of small-diameter copper tubing that will just fit through the dipstick hole. The tubing can be carefully bent to help reach the lowest part of the sump. Not only will it help get the last drop of oil, but also it will provide a convenient pumping angle without hose kinks.

129

HOMEMADE LIQUID-CONTROL MANIFOLDS

Cruisers are always concerned about having too many seacocks penetrating the hull. They also like to simplify plumbing systems by reducing the number of pumps to a minimum. In either case, ease of installation, operation, and maintenance is paramount. Liquid manifolds fulfill these criteria. Tank selection, pump-out source, fuel-filter routing, and raw-water distribution are typical manifold applications.

Ted Gordon, sailing *Candide II* on Florida's west coast, shows how to design and make your own custom manifold using copper tubing or pipe nipples and pipe couplers. Valves must be of the highest quality all-stainless or bronze with Teflon seats and seals to prevent corrosion and possible air intrusion.

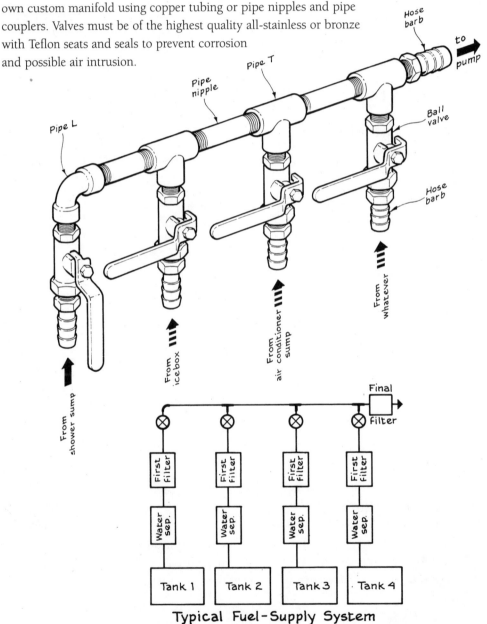

Typical Fuel-Supply System

BILGE-PUMP BACKUP

Jerry George from Anchorage, Alaska, suggests that you make your shower-sump hose long enough to be pulled out of the sump and dropped into the bilge as a secondary or backup bilge pump. A variation might be the installation of a small V-valve with one hose leading from the sump to the pump . . . the other from the bilge. Aboard Jerry's Liberty 458,

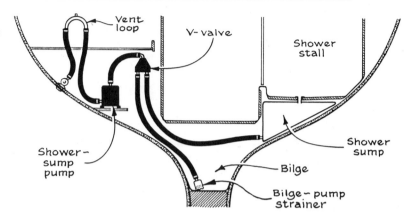

Ursa Major, each pump is on its own off/manual/automatic switch so it can be turned on manually in case of an emergency.

CLEARING FROZEN COCKPIT DRAINS

One of the northern winter plagues that affects uncovered or partially covered boats is water freezing in the cockpit drain hoses. Kenneth Brown, who sails *Dauntless*, a Tartan 33, near Waukegan, Illinois, has found an easy way to melt the ice and clear the drains. In the fall, he inserts a length of plastic tubing, allowing a couple of inches to protrude from each drain at the top and bottom. The tubing diameter should be as large as possible while allowing easy insertion into the drain. He plugs the top with a dowel or tape. Whenever the drains freeze, he unplugs the tubing, inserts a small funnel, and pours in hot water. Shortly, he is able to remove the catheter for unrestrained drainage. Before going home, he reinserts the tubes and seals them.

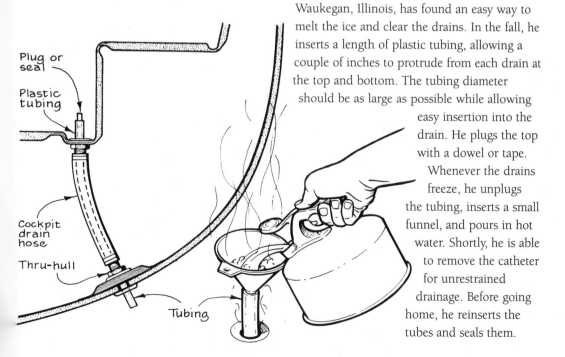

THE NUTS AND BOLTS OF NUT AND BOLT REMOVAL

Down in the dark interior of your dormant boat, some things are going to freeze . . . especially nuts and bolts. Ordinary steel parts such as those used on or near your engine are the worst, but even the lower grades of stainless fasteners can seize. So Dick Cartelli from Putney, Vermont, follows procedures that assure easy removal of even the most stubborn nut or bolt.

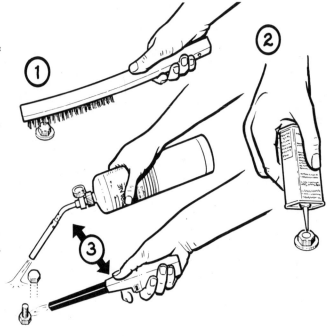

Before putting his Nautica sloop, *Beldiro*, into storage, Dick places a drop or two of penetrating oil or silicone lubricant on bolt threads where they enter nuts or metal parts. During the winter, he'll repeat this procedure on shaft-flange fasteners and bolts that enter cast iron. For fasteners that are likely to require removal during the sailing season, Dick applies Never-Seez or other preventive products to stave off the problem before it begins.

When removing stuck fasteners, Dick says:

- Use a wire brush to remove as much rust as possible (1).
- Lubricate with penetrating oil or silicone (2).
- Add heat: for nuts, a long butane barbecue lighter works well. For bolts in solid iron parts, use an LP torch on the surrounding metal. Continue to lubricate while heating (3).
- Alternate between unscrewing ¼ turn and tightening ⅛ turn. Continue to lubricate (4).
- You might need to use a little shock treatment. Tap the wrench handle with a steel or plastic hammer . . . but not too hard (5). If this doesn't get the nut or bolt started, the last resort is an impact wrench. If you don't have one, you can rent one.

PURGING FRESH WATER FOR WINTER STORAGE

Cliff and Billie Donley sail a Hunter 27 named *Celestra* out of Toledo, Ohio, where it freezes during much of the winter. The Donleys have been successful in using an inflatable-dinghy foot pump connected to a temporarily installed T-fitting for purging water from the pressure side of their freshwater system. With the pump turned off, a plastic in-line coupler is removed from the lowest point in the system and allowed to drain. Then the T-fitting is installed and air pumping forces out the remaining water by opening one spigot, drain, and outlet at a time. It is possible to provide air pressure from a vacuum cleaner, small compressor, or scuba tank.

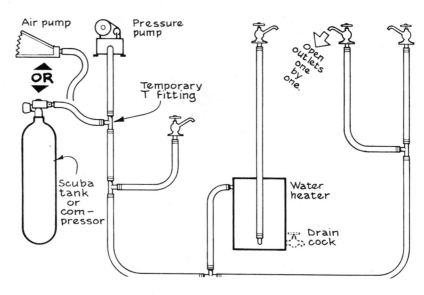

Jim McGuire from Warwick, Rhode Island, who owns a 35-foot Anastasia cutter named *Desiderata*, displaces the fresh water in his system by first draining the tanks and water heater. Next, he disconnects both from the pressure system, then places the pickup hose from the tank into a container of antifreeze solution. By opening each outlet one by one, and allowing the pump to run until antifreeze begins to flow, Jim is sure that all parts of his system, including pump, valves, and other hardware, are protected. In the spring, he refills his tank with fresh water and flushes the system several times until pure water is available from all outlets.

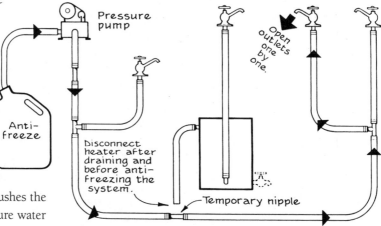

HANDGRIPS FOR BILGE-PUMP HANDLES

Now, you wouldn't think that a comfortable handle on a manual bilge pump would be a big deal, and maybe you never gave it much thought. But Ed Flanagan from Webster, New York, can tell you about the blisters and bleeding palms that result after several nonstop, panic-stricken hours of strokin' to stay afloat. Ed's pump had a hard, ball-type handle end that kept slipping off, so he decided to do without. Now he has installed two force-fit foam-rubber bicycle handle grips (sold as a pair) for two-handed, long-handled pumping.

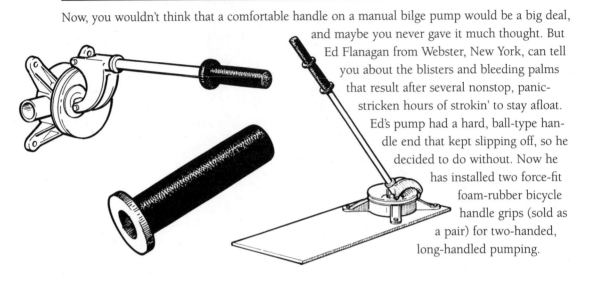

ADDING ENGINE ROOM STORAGE

Oil and fuel filters, V-belts, impellers, an extra thermostat, some special wrenches, all sorts of spare parts, some stuffing-box packing, and a flashlight are just some of the things Gerald Crowley keeps in *Lea's* engine-room storage racks. He went to his local hardware store and bought a variety of vinyl-covered wire units that he screwed to the compartment bulkheads. He also purchased an acrylic "hot file" at an office supply. It's mounted to the back of the engine-room door, and holds all the manuals that relate to the ship's mechanical equipment.

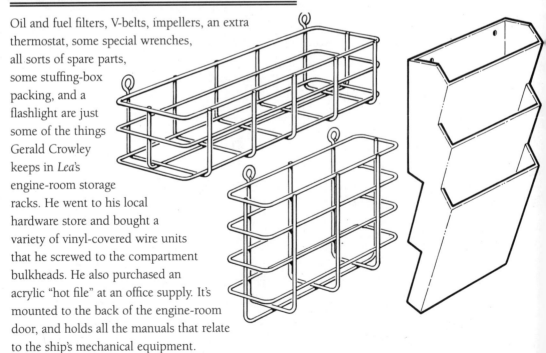

ADD A VALVE TO YOUR FUEL-WATER SEPARATOR

Most fuel-water separators are fitted with a simple, threaded drain plug. Draining off water and other fuel contaminants is a messy upside-down job that requires a wrench and X-ray vision. Staffan Svensson aboard *Swede Heart* from St. Thomas, U.S. Virgin Islands, made his life much simpler and cleaner by substituting the original plug with a brass, fuel-rated drain cock. Now draining fuel in a restricted area is done in a few seconds with a flick of the wrist without the need for special tools.

FAIL-SAFE BILGE-PUMP CIRCUITRY

After learning of several sinkings because of bilge-pump switch failures, Emil Gaynor from Camarillo, California, decided to make some modifications to the bilge-pump circuitry aboard his Cal 46 *Frenesi*. By installing an extra float switch and a push-button intermittent switch (this could also have been a toggle switch), Emil was able to increase the options for pump activation while adding an automatic backup circuit in case the primary circuit develops a problem. The backup float switch is slightly above the

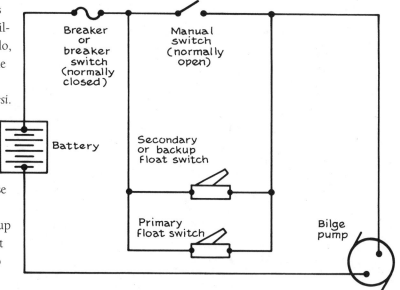

primary, thus assuring a time delay between the two. After all, if they were both located to kick in at the same bilge-water level, you might not be able to detect a defective switch.

REMOVING FLAX SHAFT-GLAND PACKING

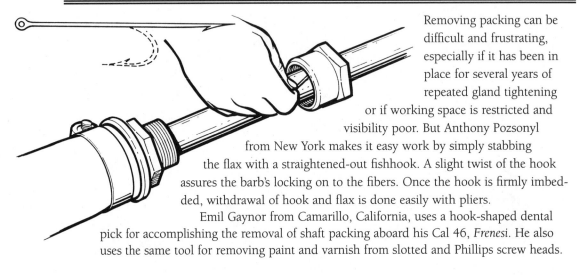

Removing packing can be difficult and frustrating, especially if it has been in place for several years of repeated gland tightening or if working space is restricted and visibility poor. But Anthony Pozsonyl from New York makes it easy work by simply stabbing the flax with a straightened-out fishhook. A slight twist of the hook assures the barb's locking on to the fibers. Once the hook is firmly imbedded, withdrawal of hook and flax is done easily with pliers.

Emil Gaynor from Camarillo, California, uses a hook-shaped dental pick for accomplishing the removal of shaft packing aboard his Cal 46, *Frenesi*. He also uses the same tool for removing paint and varnish from slotted and Phillips screw heads.

APPLYING LEVERAGE

The handles of seacocks always seem to be ridiculously short, but the better to locate the hardware in tight places such as tiny cabinets or under the engine where you can barely get your hand. So when a seacock begins to seize, you often are not able to rotate the handle without adding some mechanical advantage. Applying hammer blows should never be an option because it can result in a broken handle or dislodged or damaged seacock. But Bill and Basha Steagall from Boulder City, Nevada, who sail a custom 50-foot ketch named *Inspiration*, had a 45-degree and a 90-degree seacock wrench fabricated by a welding shop. Bill specified #4130 steel alloy tubing (bicycle tubing), but stainless steel would have provided corrosion resistance. The wrenches also could have been made from galvanized steel threaded-pipe parts, eliminating the need for welding. Now, the Steagalls can apply steadily increasing leverage to seacocks positioned in the most inaccessible places.

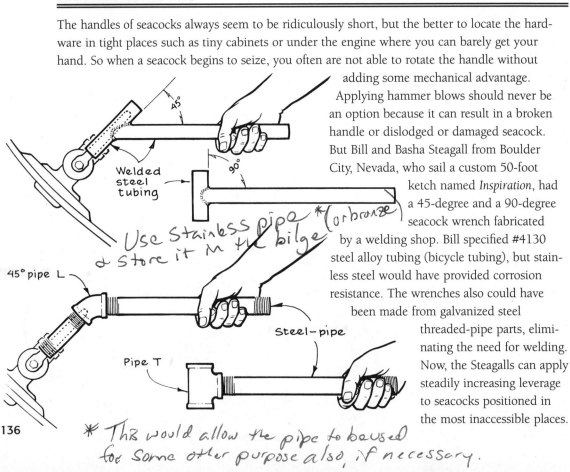

Use Stainless pipe ✱*(or bronze)*
& store it in the bilge

45° pipe L

Welded steel tubing

Steel–pipe

Pipe T

✱ *This would allow the pipe to be used for some other purpose also, if necessary.*

REMOVING STUFFING-BOX PACKING

Instead of trying to pick the packing out of the stuffing box with a bent paper clip or a screwdriver, which is a frustrating exercise, Richard Bennett from Fort Lauderdale, Florida, has suggestions that really work.

Drive a long but small-diameter self-tapping screw into the packing, then just pull it out using pliers. To make it even easier, fabricate a tool by having the screw welded to the end of a Phillips-head screwdriver.

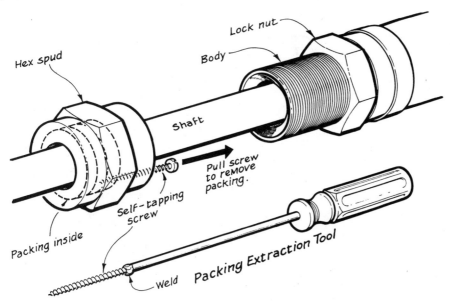

THE LAST STRAW

Aboard *Moonshadow*, Carol Elliott's Out Island 41 from Pocomoke, Maryland, the little red plastic tube that comes taped to the side of the spray-lubricant can will never disappear again. She fabricated a quiver by taping a 4-inch length of drinking straw to the side of the can. The lower end of the straw is folded over about ½ inch to form the bottom of the quiver.

Creasing the straw lengthwise will help prevent the plastic tube from falling out if the spray can is inverted. The straw can hold several plastic tubes just in case someone needs an extra.

TOPSIDE JERRICAN STORAGE IDEAS

A lot of boats doing the waterways or venturing offshore beyond their normal power-range limits carry extra fuel in jerricans. Securing them for the most adverse conditions is a real challenge. Here are three variations on the same theme by sailors with a lot of miles under their keels.

Dixon McGhie, who cruises aboard *Duet*, a Pacific Seacraft 25 from Satellite Beach, Florida, attached teak frames to the port and starboard shrouds, using bolts that pass through the open turnbuckle bodies. The 5-gallon jerricans are held down by 1-inch straps and plastic side quick-release buckles. In this arrangement, the jerricans rest on the bulwark cap to reduce infringement on the walkway. However, the frames do protrude slightly beyond the vessel's beam and might pose problems when docking alongside. Snagging sheets and torquing turnbuckles could also be drawbacks.

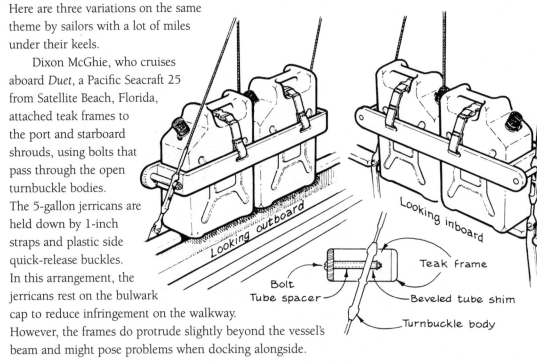

Looking outboard

Looking inboard

Bolt
Tube spacer
Teak frame
Beveled tube shim
Turnbuckle body

George Leonnig, who cruises aboard the sailing vessel *Moctobi* from Portland, Oregon, has installed long, wood strongbacks to pairs of lifeline stanchions using stainless U-bolts. Each strongback can support and store 5-gallon jerricans. The strongbacks are slotted for the passage of securing straps fabricated with quick-release side buckles. This system does infringe on side-deck walk space but reduces the possibility of sheet snagging.

U-bolt

Securing straps

U-bolt

Slots
Looking inboard

John Brand, who sails a Fantasia 35 called *Pinniped*, has installed tubing Ts to his stanchions, to which he attached custom-bent stainless restraint rails. They have been cut to fit snugly against the jerricans to prevent virtually all movement. He covers the jerricans with good-looking canvas that matches the sail covers. This prevents overheating and expansion of the fuel and protects the jerricans from UV deterioration.

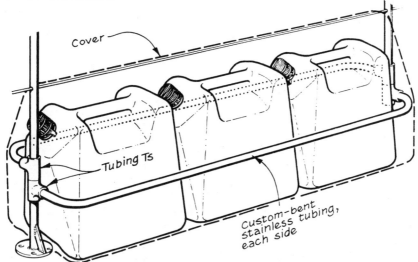

NONSPILL JERRICAN SPIGOT

If you have ever spilled fuel from the spigot of an almost-full jerrican while trying to fill an outboard, portable generator, or alcohol stove, you're not alone. It's especially difficult to hit the hole when it's rough, even if you're using a funnel, but Noel Lien, who sails a Heritage 35 sloop named *Kalinka I* from Toronto, offers hope that is simple and inexpensive. Just slip a length of ½-inch fuel-proof hose snugly onto the end of the plastic spigot. When fueling, just insert the hose into the fuel-fill hole before tilting the jerrican. This simple trick will also work when filling a mower.

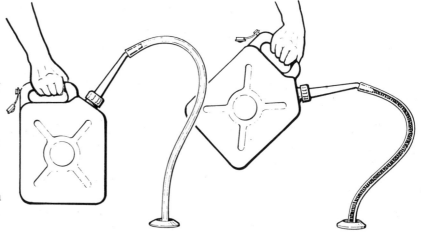

IN-WATER SEACOCK OR THRU-HULL CLEANING

Attempting to clean out a clogged seacock or thru-hull while underway is often impossible, always messy, usually very time-consuming, and sometimes very dangerous. The process often requires disconnecting hoses that are below the waterline, resulting in huge quantities of gushing seawater soaking everything while the bilge pump works feverishly to keep up with the flood. So, what's the answer?

Peter Boyle, from Bay of Islands, New Zealand, came up with a solution that might work for you. Install a length of reinforced hose to the tailpiece of the seacock or thru-hull so it reaches above the waterline. Then affix a threaded T-fitting that leads to or from the seawater appliance. Place a threaded pipe cap into the upper leg of the T to seal the assembly.

To clean a seacock or thru-hull, just remove the pipe cap and ream the obstruction with an engine-oil dipstick. Now you'll be able to clear barnacles, seaweed, and even the dreaded polyethylene-plastic bags from your important waterways.

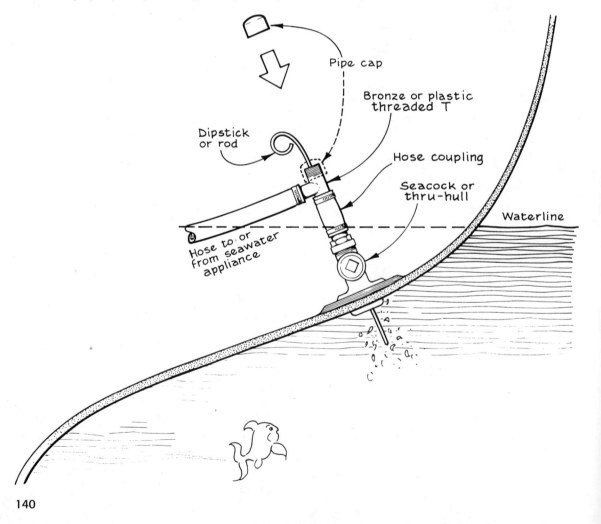

Pipe cap

Bronze or plastic threaded T

Dipstick or rod

Hose coupling

Seacock or thru-hull

Waterline

Hose to or from seawater appliance

A MODIFIED OUTBOARD CARRIER

Ken Bozarth from Daytona Beach, Florida, couldn't fit his outboard carrier into the dock box or *Sea Level*'s cockpit locker. So he cut the upright tubes, inserted wood dowels, and used bolts and wing nuts to allow quick reassembly. He also installed a removable plywood platform to the carrier's base that supports a 5-gallon bucket for the purpose of flushing the engine with fresh water.

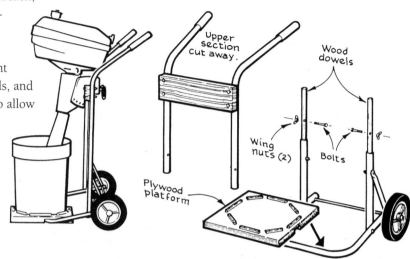

OUTBOARD SECURITY WHEN TRAILERING

Jack McKenzie didn't like the way his 82-pound outboard motor bounced around on its bracket when towing his Catalina 25. He was afraid the forces would fatigue fastenings or damage the boat's transom. So he fabricated a restraining bridle composed of a length of chain, two steel hooks, some hose, and a turnbuckle. With the outboard in the raised position, Jack passes the bridle around the back of the engine, places the hooks onto the stern cleats, and takes up on the turnbuckles until the engine is snug and immovable.

Using a lower restraint chain is also a good idea. This may be fastened to the transom by installing a pair of stainless-steel padeyes.

STANCHIONLESS OUTBOARD MOUNTING

Brian Leney from Fairfax, Virginia, wanted to install an off-the-shelf plastic outboard bracket onto the stern pulpit of his Hunter 37, *Hummer*. These brackets are grooved to fit over a T intersection made up of the horizontal rail and a vertical stanchion of the pulpit. Unfortunately, the T intersections might not be in the ideal positions for outboard storage, or the outboard might encroach on stern-rail seating or space occupied by rigging devices, LP tanks, or crew-overboard gear. If a single bracket had been installed onto the upper rail alone, it couldn't have been tightened enough to prevent it from flopping over with the weight of an outboard motor.

His solution was amazingly simple. He bought two brackets and attached one to the upper rail and the other, upside down, fits onto the lower rail. A short piece of tubing or dowel interconnects the two brackets. The brackets are absolutely rigid and the outboard is secure in any condition.

Desired outboard location

Tubing or dowel

PREVENTING BOLT SEIZURE

Threaded metal assemblies have a penchant for seizing, making disassembly difficult without destroying threads or the part itself. It is not only a problem with dissimilar metals, such as stainless steel set in aluminum, but it happens with stainless steel screwed into stainless steel and carbon steel bolts in carbon steel or iron. The solution is always to coat the threads with an antiseize compound before assembling. Such a compound is designed to resist corrosion, galling, and seizing. For engine parts, where heat is a problem, use a high-temperature antiseize compound such as Never-Seez. Turnbuckles, although not subject to high temperatures, can be coated with the same material. Screws used in the assembling of lower units of outboard motors should be coated before screwing into place. Low-temperature compounds are available for putting stainless-steel screws into aluminum spars. Never assemble threaded metal parts dry, and never use plain grease.

AN UNDERWAY FRESHWATER OUTBOARD FLUSHING SYSTEM

Outboard longevity can be drastically increased if its water cooling system is flushed with fresh water after each use. But often, pressurized fresh water is not available, especially when cruising.

Carl Daniels from Valrico, Florida, invested in a small submersible 12-volt pump, a short garden hose, a 5-gallon container, and an outboard motor flushing "earmuff" to make his system. He reports that it works great but warns that you shouldn't run your outboard in gear while it's out of the water to avoid personal injury.

Any outboard shop can recommend the correct flushing earmuff for your particular motor.

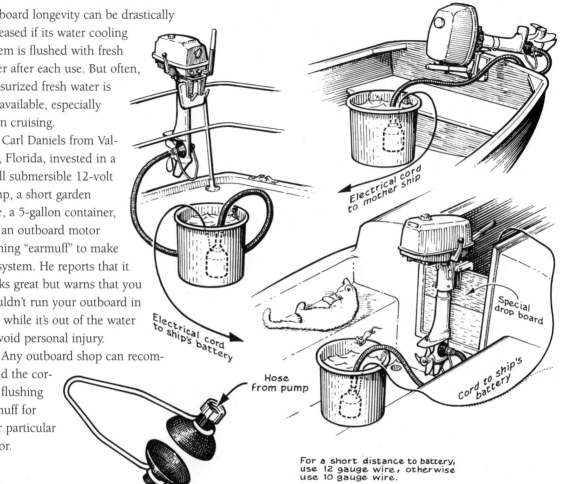

Electrical cord to mother ship

Special drop board

Electrical cord to ship's battery

Hose from pump

Cord to ship's battery

For a short distance to battery, use 12 gauge wire, otherwise use 10 gauge wire.

A SIMPLE, STRONG OUTBOARD MOUNTING BRACKET

The pulpit outboard bracket made by George Harris of Apple Valley, California, for his Tayana 37, *Sojourn*, is so simple and foolproof that it deserves attention. If you use high-quality marine lumber and stainless fasteners, the bracket will provide many years of reliable service as well as good looks. Sealing with oil or painting will increase its longevity.

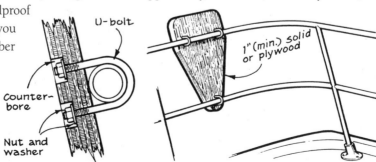

U-bolt

Counter-bore

Nut and washer

1" (min.) solid or plywood

143

TRAILER ENGINE MOUNT

Ray Henry doesn't like to leave the outboard engine on the transom of *Compromise* when she's being towed on the road. So, he fabricated and installed an extremely simple but very strong mounting bracket that can handle the engine load, no matter the roughness of the pavement or terrain. Materials included a couple of pressure-treated 2 by 8 boards, two steel U-bolts and a rubber "bow stop" with a bracket from a trailer shop, and a short length of 1½- by 1½-inch galvanized-steel angle iron. Finally, a small restraining line is passed around the shaft housing to keep the engine snugly in place when cruising down the highway.

The special U-bolts and the rubber bow stop shown in the drawing are available from a trailer distributor or repair facility.

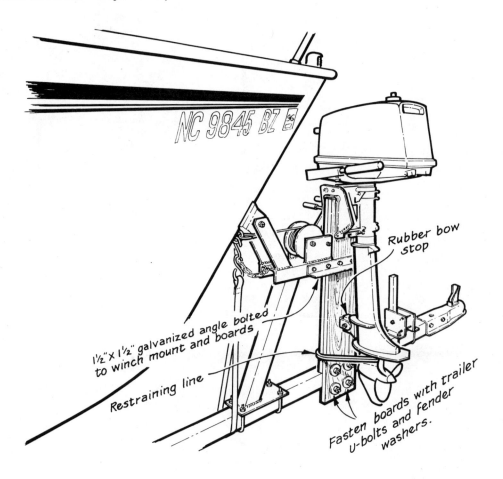

NC 9845 BZ 86

Rubber bow stop

1½" X 1½" galvanized angle bolted to winch mount and boards

Restraining line

Fasten boards with trailer U-bolts and fender washers.

CHAPTER 9

VENTILATION

Whether you live aboard or simply cruise on the weekends, ventilation is key to comfort. Fresh air in the cabin can mean the difference between a good night's sleep and a humid, restless ordeal. And keeping the musty smell out of a sailboat makes everyone happy. Here are breezy ideas for everything from louvered doors and fans in the hatches to canvas wind chutes.

ULTRASIMPLE BUG SCREENS

Just when you think you've seen all the possible bug-screen ideas, along comes an innovative approach from Emily Morse in Pound Ridge, New York, that could revolutionize the bug-barrier business.

For her Swan 43, *Blithe Spirit*, she sewed lead-shot tapes into the hems of common fine-mesh plastic screen. The lead-shot tape is available from most fabric shops for about $1 per yard, and four rows of tape are required for each hem. As an alternative, lead (not steel) buckshot from a gun shop can be poured in the ends of the hems before sewing them closed. The finished screens should be about 6 inches larger than the outside hatch dimensions. When needed, the screens are simply draped over the open hatch coamings. The weight of the lead shot will keep them in place, even in a breeze.

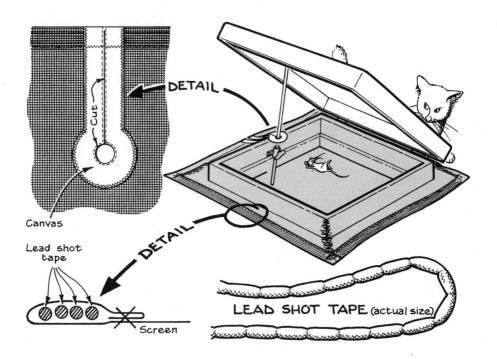

Canvas

Lead shot tape

DETAIL

DETAIL

Screen

LEAD SHOT TAPE (actual size)

Cut

FRESH AIR AND SECURITY

Jack and Pat Tyler sail their Pearson 42, called *Whish*, out of St. Petersburg, Florida. The summer nights are always humid and often still, so both solar and solar/battery-powered vents are very popular to help change out the air in closed cabins. Usually these vents are installed on or near hatches. How can you prevent a thief from simply pulling the vent out, then reaching in to open the hatch?

Jack suggests drilling small holes through both sides of the permanently installed rim and the "throat" of the vent just below the fan blades. Screw several small fasteners into both sides of the vent's base. The vent will remain in place despite lots of upward pulling on the vent from above.

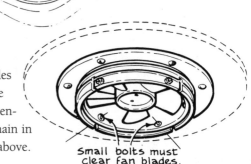

Small bolts must clear fan blades.

PROTECTING SOLAR-POWERED VENTS

Ian Cameron from Victoria, British Columbia, Canada, made a considerable investment in solar-powered vents to help keep his Cascade 36, *Carmida*, fresh and airy in his absence. He soon

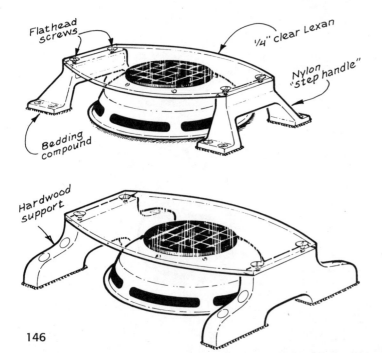

Flathead screws

¼" clear Lexan

Nylon "step handle"

Bedding compound

Hardwood support

noticed marring and scratching of the surfaces of the solar arrays. He wondered how much inadvertent abrasion and impact the units could withstand before their performance would be impaired. Without knowing the answer, he decided to protect the arrays from further damage. Ian made supporting rectangles of clear ¼-inch Lexan on pairs of legs. For these, Ian used nylon "step handles" made by Sea-Dog and priced at about $10 per vent. He suggests that the legs could also have been fashioned out of teak, ash, oak, or other hardwood to save a little money.

FLAPS DOWN . . . PREPARE FOR CROSSWIND

At one time or another, every sailor attempts to manipulate the wind so that more of it goes down the hatch to cool and ventilate the boat's interior. Raising and lowering hatches, hoisting windscoops, installing multidirectional hatch hinges, and adding canvas hatch sides are some of the techniques used to increase airflow. But Monty and Betty Nation from Palm Beach Gardens, Florida, have devised a practical and inexpensive way of controlling not only the air quantity but the air direction as well. They bought a small adjustable-louver door from a local builders' supply store and trimmed it to fit into the forward hatch of their 32-foot C-Mist, *Tandem Vincitur*. The louver unit simply rests on top of the hatch coaming interior trim piece. They gave it several coats of paint to protect the glued joints, and they cut the control rod to make possible multiple wind speed/air direction adjustments. Now Monty and Betty can individualize the airflow just by manipulating their side of the louver.

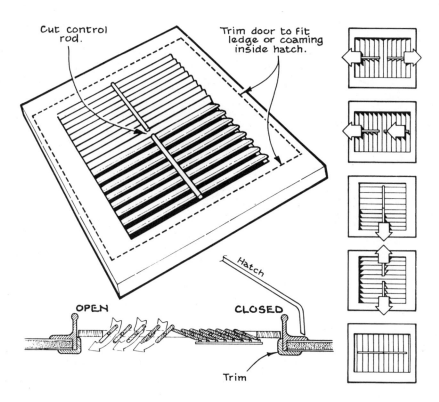

INSTALLING A FORWARD HATCH FAN

David and Jana Craft from Texarkana, Arkansas, sail their Hunter 25, *Wanna*, on Lake Ouachita, where it gets hot like you wouldn't believe. So Dave installed a removable box fan by first cutting a piece of ¾-inch plywood to just fit the hatch opening, then cutting a hole exactly the shape of the fan. The fan is attached to the wood frame with four small steel angle brackets or stainless-steel straps. To prevent the fan frame from falling through the hatch, a few small stainless straps are screwed to the frame's upper surface, overhanging about ½ inch.

　　Dave installed his fan so it exhausts air, but you can arrange yours to draw air if you wish.

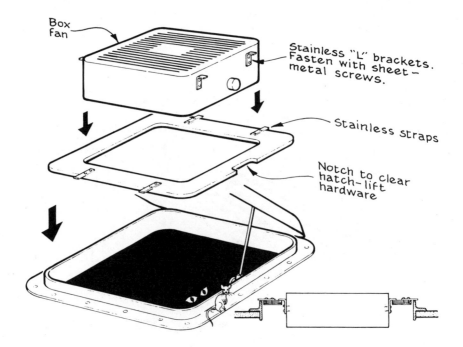

DORADE VENT CLOSURES

While many yacht manufacturers install Dorade deck and cabin vents, some do not provide interior closures to control airflow. You always have to go topside to accomplish this simple task. Gerald Crowley, sailing *Lea* out of Punta Gorda, Florida, offers several solutions that are easy to install.

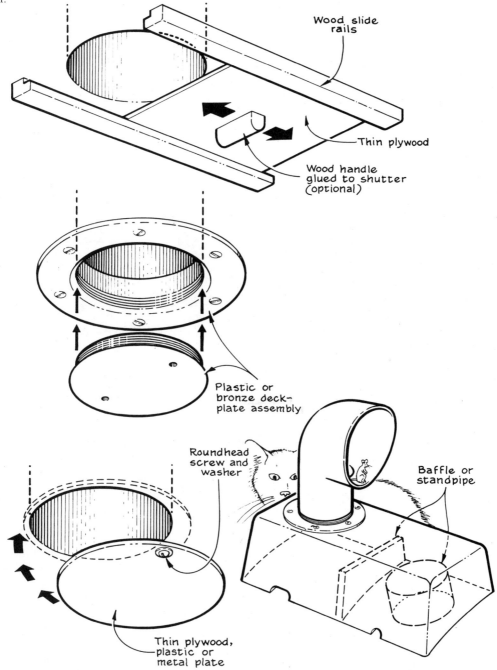

Wood slide rails

Thin plywood

Wood handle glued to shutter (optional)

Plastic or bronze deck-plate assembly

Roundhead screw and washer

Baffle or standpipe

Thin plywood, plastic or metal plate

149

DIRECTING HATCH AIRFLOW

Once fresh air has entered a hatchway, it goes wherever it wants, regardless of where you need it. This might be a chilling blast straight down on your sleeping guests or onto the chart table, sending papers flying throughout the boat. Vic Paterno from Pennsauken, New Jersey, fixed the problem aboard *Entemedor* by making lightweight cloth wind chutes that can be oriented in any direction under his lift hatches.

The geometry of the chutes is very simple. Three sides are slightly larger than the hatch coaming dimensions, while the fourth side is about a foot longer. When installed, the longer side droops down in the direction of the desired airflow. Dot snap fasteners are used to secure them in place.

An additional bonus of Vic's chutes is the added privacy below when the hatches are open.

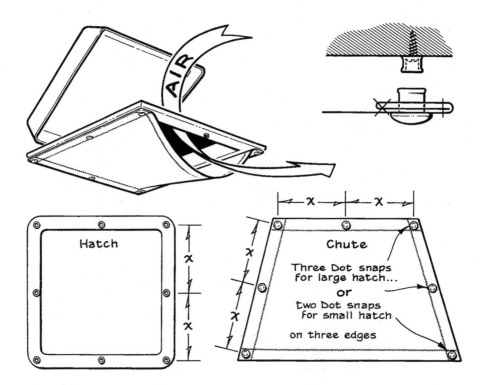

CATCHY PORTHOLE SCOOPS

Portholes never seem to contribute much ventilation unless the wind is abeam, which is rare when a boat is at anchor. While cruising eastern Central America and Venezuela aboard *Bristol Blue*, Derek and Sally Gardner decided to solve this problem. They made unusual, but extremely efficient, porthole windscoops using light canvas, Dot snap fasteners, some PVC pipe (which could have been wood dowel), and a little bit of ⅛-inch cord.

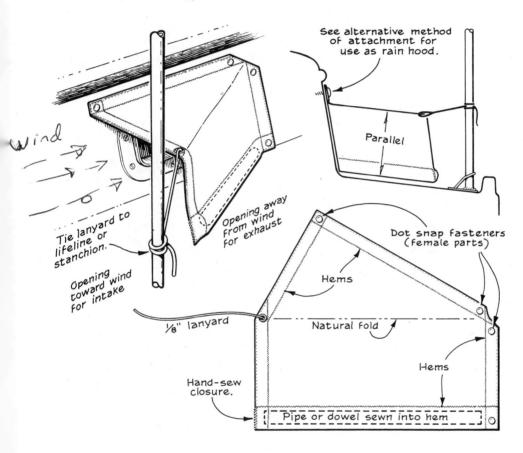

The windscoop pattern is quite simple, but it's recommended that you make a folded cardboard model to make sure it fits correctly before cutting your material. The windscoop direction can be reversed by swapping port for starboard. The lower outboard corner is not secured as this allows the back of the scoop to open when a strong gust hits, thus acting as a pressure relief valve.

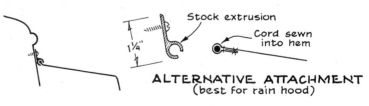

ALTERNATIVE ATTACHMENT
(best for rain hood)

PERMANENTLY INSTALLED HINGED HATCH SCREENS

Robert St. Martin made ridged frames for his hatch screens using inexpensive picture molding (see Mitred Corner section in illustration), fastening the screen material with inner wood strips. The finished frames are attached to the cabin overhead with pairs of hinges at one end and hooks-and-eyes at the other. He painted his assemblies to match *Escapade's* overhead, but if made to match the boat's trim wood, they could have been oiled or varnished.

If your cabin overhead is curved in the area of your hatches, you must install beveled blocks under the fixed halves of the hinges, thus aligning the hinge pins to prevent strain on the fastenings. The upper edges of the hatch frames should also be cut to fit the curve of the cabin, and this might require you to make your own frame molding. The sealing strip is optional. Of course, construction variations are possible to fit your available tools and capabilities.

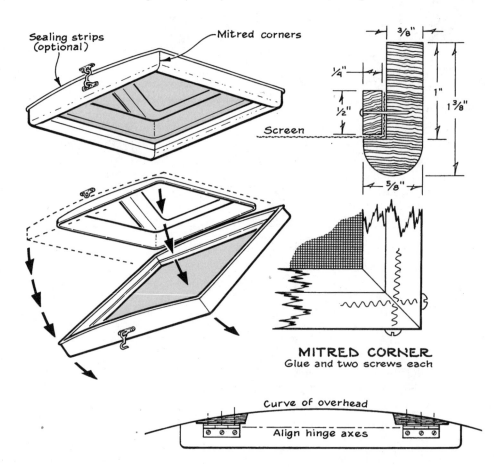

MITRED CORNER
Glue and two screws each

CHAPTER 10

GIZMOS, GADGETS, AND NIFTY IDEAS

Here's where our readers really hit their stride with all manner of suggestions for making life afloat more comfortable, safe, or efficient. Enjoy the benefit of many hours of thinking from amateur inventors, and try their ideas for everything from clotheslines and handholds to carrying jugs and mixing epoxy.

SMOOTH AS A BABY'S BOTTOM

Stuart Miller from Marblehead, Massachusetts, always wants to get the most out of his Hans Christian 33, *Quacker Jacque III*. So whenever he hauls out for the annual bottom job, he always sands the bottom to remove "dead" paint and to knock down orange peel and brush marks. The sanding also reduces unnecessary paint buildup. In the past, Stuart used a heavy electric sander, and it was an exhausting and dusty job. Always being so close to the work also posed a hazard from the toxic dust cloud, and it worried him.

Today, Stuart's bottom sanding is still exhausting and dusty, but it's not nearly as bad as it used to be. He now uses a swiveling, drywall sandpaper holder attached to a mop or screw-in broom handle. Stuart says it's actually faster than power sanding and usually requires less strenuous posture. The best part is that he no longer has to stand in the bottom-paint fallout.

WHAT'S KNOT TO LOVE?

In Clifford Ashley's day, it was common to fashion beautiful, knotted lanyards for all sorts of uses aboard a sailing ship. William Smothers from Peoria, Illinois, has rediscovered that marlinspike artistry of old, finding all sorts of modern-day uses for these traditional knots found in *Ashley's Book of Knots* and other decorative-knot books. More specifically, he tied all sorts of button knots and two-stranded lanyard knots in various colors using ⅛- to ³⁄₁₆-inch polyester braided line. Most of the knots took on the form of lanyards used for shackle pulls aboard his Clipper 26, others became drawer pulls, and some long ones made of bungee cord are used as sail ties; many wound up as key chains, bell pulls, knife and tool lanyards, and toggle ties for hanging coils of line and seizing coils of hose and electrical cord. Using the smaller-line diameter, he produced colorful zipper pulls for jackets and foul-weather gear. Bill is now replacing the sail-bag lanyards with new, colorful ties featuring beautifully knotted ends.

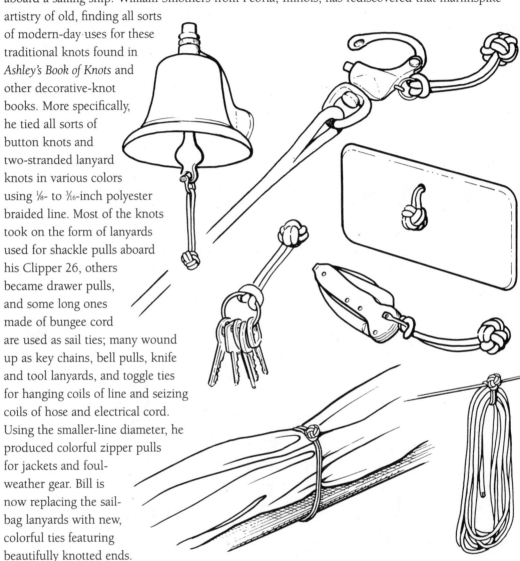

The knotted lanyards shown in these sketches are made with a double knife lanyard knot (sometimes called a "marlinspike lanyard knot," "two-strand diamond knot," or "bosun's whistle knot"). Many other ornate knots would do just as well and are equally fun to tie.

VITAL HAULOUT EQUIPMENT

Geoff Potter and Phoebe Douglass from San Francisco didn't want the boatyard ladder to mar their Baba 35's topsides. So they sliced a couple of tennis balls and fit them over the upper ends of the ladder rails to protect *Bidarka's* gelcoat. They also make it a habit to tie the ladder tightly to the lifeline stanchions to prevent it from slipping and to discourage "borrowing."

NO MORE STAINS

Boats, especially white ones, take on a brownish beard at the bow after venturing along inland waterways. This is caused by tannin, a natural chemical produced by trees and bushes. Wolfgang Scheuer from Fronreute, Germany, says this stain can be removed simply by washing the hull with lemon slices. This method can also remove light rust stains without damaging gelcoat or paint.

MOVABLE FIDDLES

Movable fiddles should fit easily into any position regardless of which end is forward. The trick to drilling perfectly matching peg holes is the use of an accurately made drilling jig. Metal is best, but hardwood will do. The width of the jig should match the thickness of your fiddles. Bore the jig holes on a drill press if possible. Be sure that the holes are perfectly centered: a center punch will help. Fiddle pegs should be no more than 2 feet apart, so a 4-foot fiddle will have three pegs.

- Securely tape or clamp the jig to the edge of the fiddle. Insert the drill into the jig hole, drilling into the fiddle at high speed but with little pressure until the stop has been reached (1).
- Remove the drill and insert a peg. Drill the second hole in the same way without disturbing the jig (2).
- To drill a third hole, untape or unclamp the jig, end-for-end the jig around the peg, then retape or reclamp it to the fiddle. Now drill your last hole (3).
- The pegs may be wood or metal with each end rounded. Only one drop of glue or epoxy is needed to hold them in place (4).

To drill the matching holes into the table or work top, follow the same procedure. Enlarge these holes slightly with rolled-up sandpaper so the pegs will fit easily.

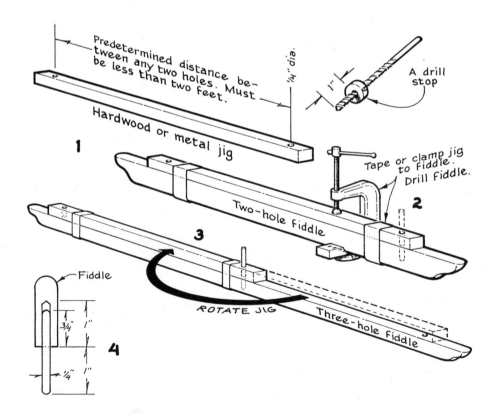

A VERY SIMPLE WATERLINE SCRUBBER

Rich Ulrich knows how exhausting it can be to scrub *Start-N-Over's* waterline from the dock or dinghy while in the prone position. Then he discovered that buoyancy added to a long brush handle can provide the necessary upward pressure to help get the job done with a lot less effort.

First, he bored a hole through a block of urethane foam and slipped it onto the brush handle. It worked! Then he tried attaching a small boat fender by looping the fender pendant around the brush handle. It worked too! Yahoo . . . a boat-scrubbing breakthrough!

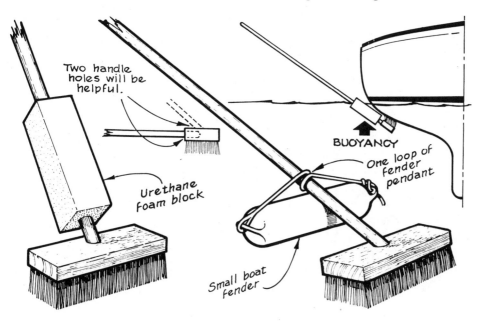

Two handle holes will be helpful.

Urethane foam block

BUOYANCY

One loop of fender pendant

Small boat fender

DUST BUSTERS

Louvered cabinet doors are great for providing ventilation for lockers, staterooms, and storage spaces, but they are a nightmare to clean. Judy and Stu Miller from Marblehead, Massachusetts, aboard their Hans Christian 33, *Quacker Jacque III*, have come up with a ridiculously simple dusting and washing technique. Just use a foam paintbrush. It won't scratch the wood, and it costs just about a dollar. Choose the brush size based on the louver spaces.

JUGGLING JERRICANS AND OTHER WEIGHTY THINGS

Dan Webster and Mary Spencer from Flint, Michigan, sail a 38-foot custom French steel cutter called *Life's Dream* on the Great Lakes. Sometimes they are not able to anchor or moor close to towns and shopping, and often the roads back to the boat are poor or nonexistent. So carrying bags of groceries or jerricans of fuel and water poses a very big problem. Recently, Dan and Mary saw a "portage yoke" in a canoe and camping catalog and thought it might be the answer to lifting their loads. A week and $15 later, a beautiful varnished ash yoke arrived, and it was perfect.

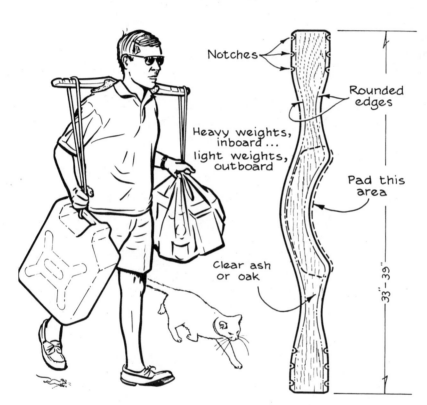

Notches

Rounded edges

Heavy weights, inboard ...
light weights, outboard

Pad this area

Clear ash or oak

33"–39"

Dan added some padding to the center area where it fits around the neck (the yoke could have been ordered with the padding for $5 more), and he cut shallow notches at the ends to capture the lifting lanyards. Now, Dan and Mary can travel several miles with a porter-style load that would have bogged them down before in less than a hundred yards.

HOMEMADE VIEWING BUCKET

When Vicki Sielaff aboard *Meridian* realized that she had lent her much-needed clear-bottom viewing bucket to a sailing friend, she simply made a new one. By rounding up commonly available inexpensive materials and investing about an hour of time, she was quickly back in business. The cost was about $10, and the satisfaction worth a million!

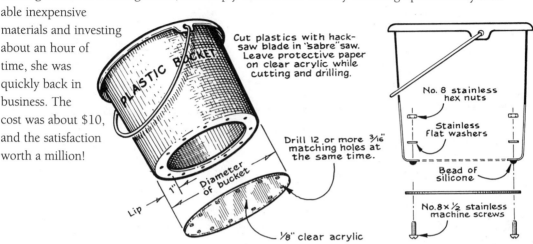

Cut plastics with hack-saw blade in 'sabre" saw. Leave protective paper on clear acrylic while cutting and drilling.

Drill 12 or more 3/16" matching holes at the same time.

No. 8 stainless hex nuts

Stainless flat washers

Bead of silicone

No. 8 x 1/2 stainless machine screws

Diameter of bucket

1"

Lip

1/8" clear acrylic

SOLAR-SHOWER UPGRADE

The portable, plastic-bag solar shower that we are all familiar with is sold with a notoriously short hose. The shower head is not very efficient, and the water turn-on mechanism is unwieldy.

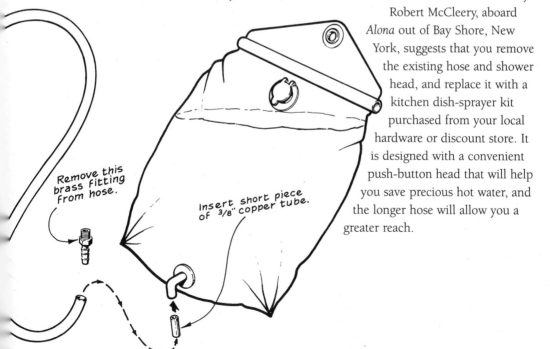

Robert McCleery, aboard *Alona* out of Bay Shore, New York, suggests that you remove the existing hose and shower head, and replace it with a kitchen dish-sprayer kit purchased from your local hardware or discount store. It is designed with a convenient push-button head that will help you save precious hot water, and the longer hose will allow you a greater reach.

Remove this brass fitting from hose.

Insert short piece of 3/8" copper tube.

159

SHOP BUT DON'T DROP

From time to time, most cruisers end up carrying plastic grocery bags over long distances. How many bags and for how long they are carried depends largely on one's technique. Pat Trimbell from Orange Park, Florida, uses "shop sticks" that allow her to tote perhaps eight bags in each hand for a mile at a time! Double that when her sailing companion, Don, is along.

A shop stick is a 7-inch length of broom handle or dowel that is carved with indents at each end and sanded smooth. The handles of the bags are looped over the indents at each end and don't slip off. How many bags are carried is up to the individual.

Pat and Don sail a 37-foot Prout Snowgoose catamaran named *Laura Lee*, hailing from Ames, Iowa. They have made dozens of shop sticks for cruising friends and often emblazon them with their boats' names.

INSTANT PRIVACY

Anna and Frank Huml, who sail a Capri 26 named *Ebb Tide* from Sturgeon Bay, Wisconsin, have solved the problem of maintaining privacy below while dockside without impairing direct lighting when they want it. They put four small self-adhesive Velcro fuzzy dots at the corners of each port and the corresponding Velcro dots on thin, frosted, vinyl sheets cut to the shapes of the ports. Very thin translucent acrylic also would have worked. It takes only a second to install or remove the coverings, which are stowed under cushions.

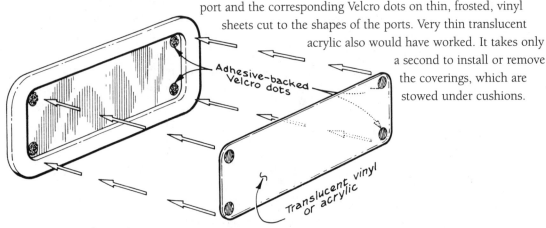

Adhesive-backed Velcro dots

Translucent vinyl or acrylic

A CRUISER'S CLOTHESLINE

Pinning clothes and towels to a lifeline might work in a pinch, but even the upper wire is too low to be really practical. And if some item is blown loose, chances are it will drop into the drink. There is also the risk of clothes becoming rust spotted. Judy Speary from Bedford, Pennsylvania, solves clothes hanging aboard *Janus*, a Whitby 42, by hanging a custom-made clothesline rig that can be suspended over the deck or cabin in a number of positions and directions. Because the unit has five parallel clotheslines, it uses very little space. For storage, the rig is rolled up and stuffed into the lazarette.

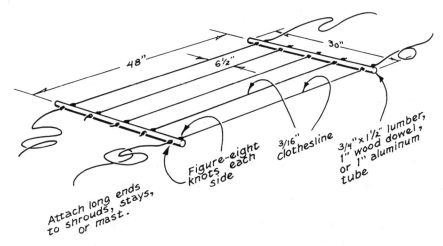

A SIMPLE DRY-CHEMICAL EXTINGUISHER CHECK

Dave Nofs, a retired firefighter, suggests that when you check your fire-extinguisher gauges for fullness, hold your dry-chemical bottles next to your ear. Tilt the bottle upside down. You should hear, and maybe feel, the chemical powder shift. If you don't hear it, this indicates that the chemical has settled or caked on the bottle sides. Tap the sides of the bottle to dislodge the powder, then rotate the bottle in all directions several times to redistribute the chemical. This is what Dave does aboard his little sloop, *Fia*, sailing from Holmes Beach, Florida.

NONPERMANENT CHART MARKERS

Spotting your position on a chart at a glance, and then moving that position in a split second is as simple as using a 3M Post-It Tape Flag. Tape Flags come in a variety of colors and sizes and are packed in handy little plastic dispensers. The Tape Flag can be applied and reapplied on your chart many times and will not damage the chart in any way.

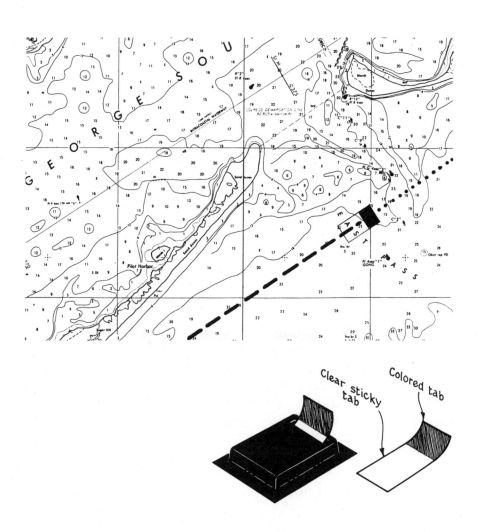

SAFETY LINE FOR TOOLS

To prevent tools from getting away when you go aloft, it's wise to attach lanyards to them. A falling screwdriver might reach speeds of over 50 mph before hitting the deck or a person. But few sailors think about tools going overboard when working on deck.

Ed Schweizer, who sails *Sea Jay*, a Catalina 27 out of Dana Point, California, has seized small rings to all his tools. He keeps pendants of various lengths handy so each tool can be tethered as it is used. One of his most vital tools is the cable cutter that would be used for dismasting under extreme weather and sea conditions. This tool has a permanent, dedicated pendant.

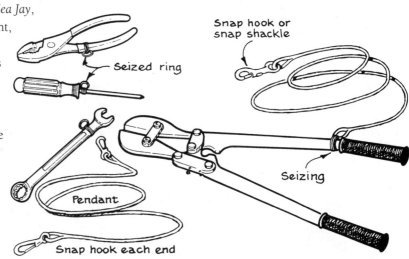

BINOCULAR LENS-CAP LANYARDS

All binoculars are supplied with lens caps, but often they are not provided with the means of keeping them tethered to prevent loss. Roger Sweet, who sails *Buck-Weet* out of Marathon, Florida, spent 5 minutes but no money to make lens-cap lanyards. All he did was pierce the soft plastic covers with a sail needle, threading twine through each. A figure-eight knot is tied on the lens side of each cover, and the bitter ends are tied to the binoculars. If your lens covers are made of a hard plastic, Roger suggests using a red-hot wire to pierce the surface.

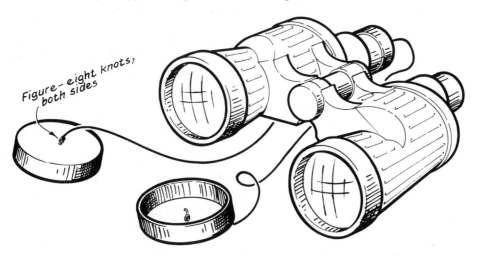

SLIPPIN' AND SLIDIN'

If you've ever washed your settee or berth cushions or made your own cushion covers, you know how difficult it is to get the covers back on. Making it more of a hassle is the fact that the cushions are usually larger than the covers. Elizabeth and Bob Fellner, who cruise in a custom motor sailer from London, Ontario, Canada, called *Chantey II*, offer two methods that will eliminate frustration.

Wrap the cushion completely with a very thin (2 mil or less) plastic drop sheet. Secure and seal the plastic with clear tape. Your foam slab will slip into its cover with ease.

The other method is to spray the cushion with "dry silicone lubricant" that can be found at most upholstery shops. But keep in mind that this is a distinctly different product from that used on turnbuckles and snap shackles. It dries in just a few seconds and is odorless.

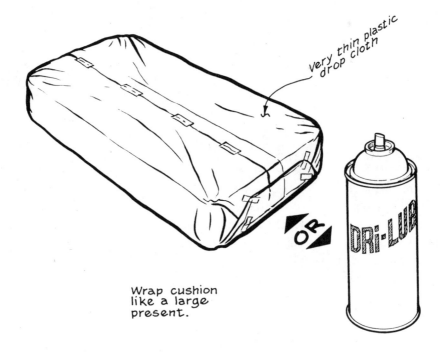

very thin plastic
drop cloth

Wrap cushion
like a large
present.

STOP LIP DRIP

If your boat's porthole spigots collect
water after a rain, as do those
aboard *Simple Gifts*, try Jay Knoll's
solution. Affix a short length of
½-inch lantern wick to the lowest
part of the spigot using a little
contact cement. Posi-
tion the inboard end
of the wick so it doesn't
interfere with the port
seal, and let it pass over
the outboard edge of
the spigot and
down the cabin
trunk a short distance.

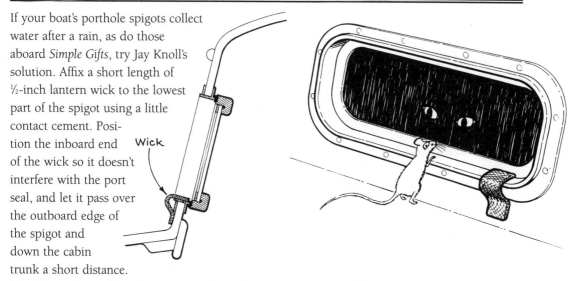

Wick

Capillary action will wick water away from the port in an amazingly short time. You won't have
to bail or drain your ports into a pan ever again.

NO-SNAP HANDRAIL AND RAIL-CAP COVERS

Saving your brightwork is best done by covering it up to prevent UV
breakdown. But, chances are, covers won't be used unless
they're convenient and easy to make. Candace Allen
from Seattle seems to have met both criteria by
designing a system that does not require
the installation of snaps. Instead,
she uses small retaining
hoops made from
schedule 20 PVC pipe.
By not attempting to fit
each covering piece
snugly, she has achieved
ultimate simplicity with
her design.

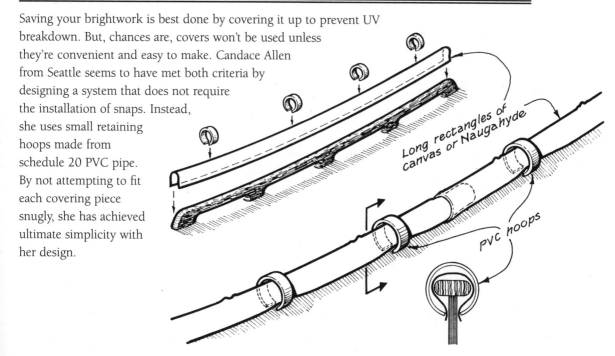

Long rectangles of
canvas or Naugahyde

PVC hoops

CLOSING THE GAP

Boats with pintle and gudgeon-hung rudders often have an open gap at the base of the rudder and keel. This gap is notorious for snagging kelp, fish nets, lobster and crab pot lines, and anchor rodes. To prevent these poten-tially dangerous and certainly inconvenient hang-ups, it is necessary to install a "heel" bar at the aft end of the keel. Dana Le Tourneau from Granada Hills, California, installed one on *Aeolian*. It is made out of two thicknesses of bronze plate that required cutting and bending but not welding or braz-ing. Your own boat might be better fit with an alternative fabrication.

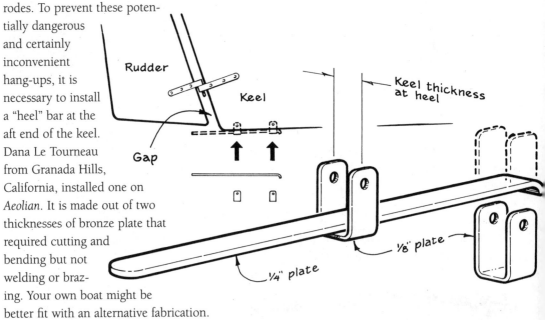

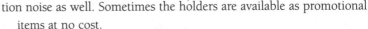

NO MORE STAIN

Kay Owens and Todd Cain from Atlanta discovered that placing steel containers such as silicone sprays, shaving cream, and bug repellent into insulated drink holders eliminates ugly circular rust stains aboard their Down Easter 32, *Kay-Tee*. They also inhibit skidding and cut down on vibra-tion noise as well. Sometimes the holders are available as promotional items at no cost.

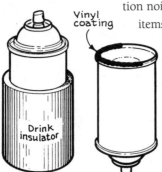

Aboard *Whish*, a Pearson 42 from St. Petersburg, Florida, Pat and Jack Tyler apply a little liquid vinyl to cut down on nasty rust rings, vibration, and slippage. They use brands sold for either coating tool handles, sealing electrical connections, or whipping lines. They say that all work equally well. To apply, they use an inexpensive artist's brush and clean up with lacquer thinner. Most steel containers stowed on shelving have been sparingly vinylized when they're brought aboard.

PAINT-CAN GUTTER DRAINAGE

When you pour paint or other coatings from the can, the gutter tends to fill with material. This makes recapping of the can messy, and prevents a good seal. Jim McGuire on *Desiderata* from Warwick, Rhode Island, suggests punching a few holes in the gutter with a small nail to allow the material to flow back into the can. Be sure to wipe the gutter clean before replacing the lid.

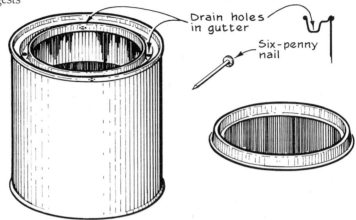

FLOORBOARD FIX

John Aklonis, who cruises aboard *Silke*, a Hans Christian 38, was worried about flying floorboards and bilge contents in the event of a rollover. Imagine the possible damage that could be done by tools, canned goods, chain, and spare parts being tossed into the cabin at high speeds during violent weather. While preparing for an extensive offshore trek, John decided to eliminate this potential problem in a way that wouldn't decrease stowage convenience.

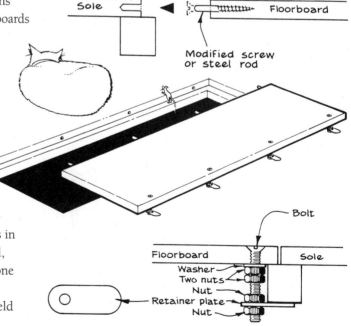

John inserted several stainless pins fashioned from large screws along each floorboard, then drilled accurately matching holes in the floor edge. When the floorboard is closed, the pins are inserted into the holes, locking one side of the board in place.

The opposite edge of the floorboard is held closed by retainers made with stainless bolts, nuts, a washer, and a rotating ⅛-inch plate. This distance between the plate and the floorboard is adjustable to assure a snug fit when the board is in position. A screwdriver is required to remove the boards for storage access, but the added safety is worth it.

SMALL-BATCH EPOXY MIXING

Measuring accurate volumes of component parts for very small batches of liquid epoxies is not possible with commonly used pumps, and measuring spoons are sometimes too large.

Gerald Crowley, sailing *Lea* out of Punta Gorda, Florida, suggests dipping a small, clean stick into component A and letting it drain until the flow is reduced to single drops. Move the stick to a small mixing cup, and count the desired number of drops as they fall.

With a second clean stick, repeat the procedure for the second epoxy component. The number of drops of each component will always be in the same ratio as called for by the epoxy manufacturer.

With a third clean stick or stirrer, mix the components, adding any desired fillers if applicable.

When measuring thick fluids from tubes, squeeze out a length of component A. Then squeeze out a length of component B that appears to be equal to the mix ratio called for by the manufacturer. Alternatively, you can squeeze out a number of equal lengths of component B that conform to the required mix.

When dipping thick epoxy components from cans, place equally sized blobs of both components onto a mixing board. The number of blobs of each component should match the required mix ratio.

LIFELINE CHAFE PREVENTION

Lifelines, as the name clearly suggests, are intended to save your life by keeping you aboard. Careful inspection will probably reveal cracking and wear of the vinyl covering where the lifelines pass through the stanchions or where they are subjected to chafe by sheets. Rust staining is clear evidence of wire corrosion and decay.

To protect their valuable lifelines, Stuart and Judy Miller, aboard *Quacker Jacque III* from Marblehead, Massachusetts, installed short lengths of snap-on, plastic shroud covering in the areas that needed attention.

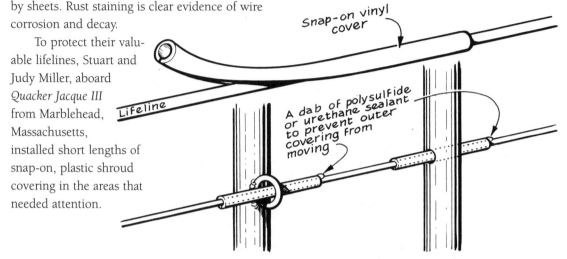

Snap-on vinyl cover

Lifeline

A dab of polysulfide or urethane sealant to prevent outer covering from moving

BRUSH PRESERVATION

Almost nothing will ruin a brush as quickly or severely as letting it dry. Even if you think you've cleaned your brush thoroughly, pockets and particles of paint remain that will granulate when the brush is reused, resulting in grit in your next finishing job.

To help prevent this problem after cleaning, work a nonevaporating fluid such as petroleum jelly, cooking oil, margarine, or clean lubricating oil deeply into the bristle. Shape the bristles, then seal in plastic wrap or aluminum foil.

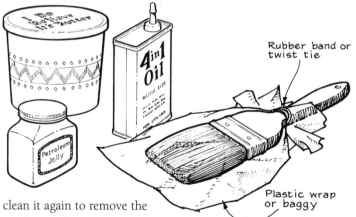

Rubber band or twist tie

4 in 1 Oil

Petroleum Jelly

Plastic wrap or baggy

To reuse the brush, clean it again to remove the fluid, and let it air dry. Petroleum jelly, cooking oil, and margarine can be removed with soap and water, but use a paint thinner if you've saved the bristles with lube oil.

AN OUNCE OF PREVENTION

When the deck closures for water fills, fuel fills, and holding-tank pumpouts are from the same manufacturer, chances are they will look and feel the same and will require the same opening tool. The only difference will be the name of the closure stamped or cast into it, but often not read. The risk of pumping the wrong fluid into a tank is very high without some additional reminder when opening each fill. Pat England from Ann Arbor, Michigan, saw what can happen while cruising aboard her boat, *Paradigm*. One boat pumped water into the fuel tank; another filled the holding tank with diesel!

To help avoid this problem, Pat made all new fill caps using 1½-inch PVC male-threaded sewer-pipe cleanout plugs. Each plug has been refashioned to require a different tool or wrench size. Additionally, she has painted each closure with a different color as an added precaution.

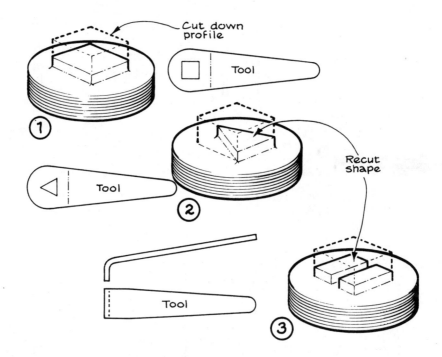

FINGER SAVERS

Aboard Frank Browning's *Gannet* from Surry, Maine, there are a half dozen or so plastic inspection plates (the kind with the molded-in finger recesses) installed on tanks, small compartment fronts, and over a bilge-pump handle socket. When the plates have been screwed tightly shut, they're a bugger to open, especially when your hands are cold. Frank solved the problem by making this simple wood deck-plate key. Now he can close the deck plates tighter and open them a lot easier. Then he devised a smaller, two-handed metal key for his fuel and water fill caps using some aluminum plate, bolts, and nuts.

LOOSENING STUCK SCREWS

Sometimes, you just can't get a screw to turn after it has been in wood for a long time. This is most frustrating when it results in a stripped screw head or broken shank. Ames Swartsfager, sailing his CT41 ketch, *Butterfly*, out of New Orleans, shares a solution that rarely fails when he works on his teak decks and interior joinery. Using a cotton swab or small eyedropper, just place a few drops of cola around the head of the screw and wait about a minute for it to soak into the wood. Apparently, the cola acts like a penetrating lubricant that also dissolves some of the oxidized metal. Whatever the chemistry, it's worth a try without risk of permanent stains.

FIGHTING OFF THE CHILL

Using a turned-on lightbulb to prevent temperatures from falling below freezing in small compartments is not a new trick. It is a popular winter antifreezing technique in the southern and mid-Atlantic states where subzero temperatures sometimes occur only at night and occasionally during short daylight periods. However, such a technique should not be used as a first line of defense against freezing in the more northerly latitudes.

Jill and Greg Delezynski from Powder Springs, Georgia, made a simple thermostat set at about 34° that can control several lightbulbs simultaneously at one or various locations aboard their Nor'Sea 27, *Guenevere*. The entire system is composed of a multisocket extension cord, one (or several) work lights with appropriate long-life bulbs, an electric heater two-wire thermostat purchased at a large builder's-supply outlet, and a switch/connecter box. In total, they spent less than $35.

The thermostat cut-in temperature can be adjusted by comparing it with a thermometer reading the desired temperature.

Jill and Greg check their boat at least several times a week, and always on days that approach the freezing point.

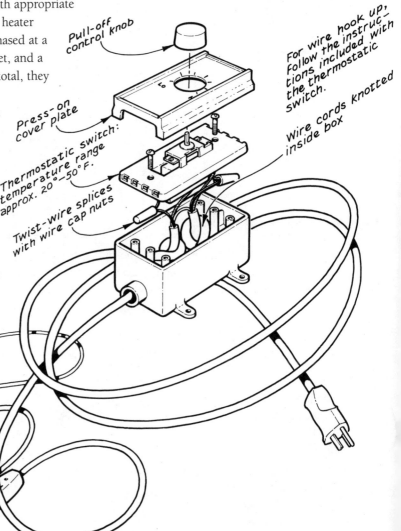

Pull-off control knob

For wire hook up, follow the instructions included with the thermostatic switch.

Press-on cover plate

Wire cords knotted inside box

Thermostatic switch: temperature range approx. 20°–50°F.

Twist-wire splices with wire cap nuts

INSTANT HANDHOLDS

Anticipation is Jeff Gross's Ericson 30 from Indian Harbour Beach, Florida. Jeff wanted to install overhead handholds, but he is fairly tall and was concerned about permanently decreased head-room. Most of his sailing is on the normally placid Indian River with occasional treks offshore.

Jeff's solution was to install stainless eye bolts into the transverse bulkheads as well as the cabin ends. The exposed threaded ends of the bolts were finished off with acorn nuts for safety and appearance. Between the eyebolts are stretched ⅝-inch lines, eye spliced at each end. One end is fitted with a snap hook while the other is fitted with a pelican hook to pull the line very tight. When not in use, the handholds are stowed in a small canvas bag.

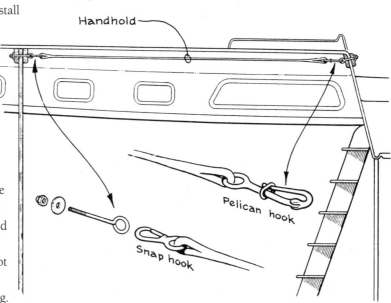

ENLARGING A HOLE

Jim McGuire from Warwick, Rhode Island, installed some larger thru-hull fittings aboard *Desiderata*, an Anastasia 32. But using a circular hole saw to enlarge the original apertures posed a problem. You see, most hole saws require use of an integral central pilot drill for accurate cutting. What to do? Jim's solution was to insert a wood damage-control plug into each hole, mark it and cut it to correct length, then apply 5-minute epoxy to seal it in place. Once this epoxy had cured, he drilled the new holes as if the old holes had never existed.

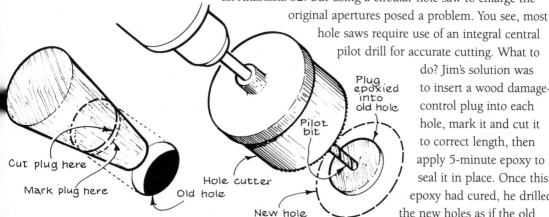

173

TAMING A WINDMILL

Many wind generators are hoisted from a headsail halyard and suspended in the boat's foretriangle, being partly stabilized by a pair of downhauls. However, the upper end of the generator is usually allowed to swing while the blade arc establishes an inefficient angle.

Dave Nofs, who has cruised the Caribbean aboard *Fia*, wrestled with these problems and finally came up with an interesting solution. He fabricated a restraining pendant that clips to the generator at one end while the other end is looped around the headsail furling gear. The loop is threaded with about a dozen practice golf balls that allow the loop to slide easily on the furled sail. Once the generator is in position, the downhauls are tightened.

Dave suggests that if your headstay is bare, a snap hook will work in place of the loop. He also says that large wood beads from a crafts shop are an alternative to golf balls.

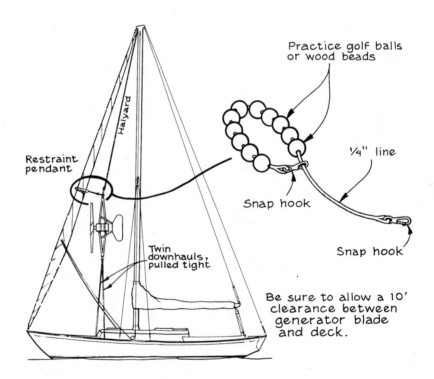

Practice golf balls
or wood beads

¼" line

Restraint
pendant

Halyard

Snap hook

Twin
downhauls,
pulled tight

Snap hook

Be sure to allow a 10'
clearance between
generator blade
and deck.

SMOOTHING COMPOUNDS

Silicone sealants, polysulfides, polyurethanes such as 3M 5200, and most epoxy repair compounds are sticky substances that are messy to work with. Gwen Bylund from Ontario, California, offers a trick to make your task easier, cleaner, and nicer looking.

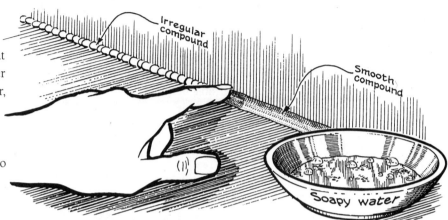

After applying the sealant or compound, dip your finger into a solution of soapy water, then sculpt or smooth the compound to desired shape. Make sure that you don't get soapy water on the surfaces to which you intend to apply the compound.

REMOTE-CONTROLLED SEALANT APPLICATION

Sometimes you just can't get the sealant gun into a small space where it's needed . . . and sometimes obstructions prevent aligning the sealant-gun spigot at the correct angle; often, holding the sealant gun awkwardly turns an easy job into an exhausting one. Michael Goulet from Québec, who sails a 34-foot Islander sloop called *Island Home*, suggests you try his solution for getting around these problems. Force a length of vinyl tubing onto the spigot, holding it in place with some seizing wire. You'll be able to apply sealant almost anywhere.

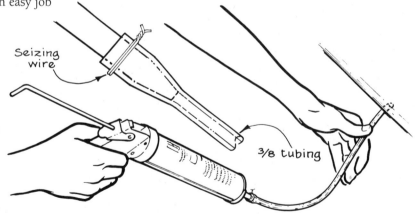

MATCHING NONSKID GELCOAT REPAIR

You probably have had to make gelcoat repairs on nonskid deck areas. And you probably have discovered the virtual impossibility of matching the nonskid pattern. Well, Simon Dresner from Spring Valley, New York, has found a way.

First, make a mold of a small, level nonskid area. Do this by building a dike using children's modeling clay. Spray the area with a pure silicone, then fill the enclosed area with liquid silicone to a depth of about ¼ inch. When the silicone has cured, simply peel up the mold.

When repairing a nonskid area, carefully apply just enough of the correct color of gelcoat to fill the divot. Spray your flexible mold with pure silicone as a release agent, then place the mold over the gelcoat so the patterns line up. Gently press the mold into the new gelcoat. Weight the mold evenly with a plastic bag full of sand. When the gelcoat cures, pull away the mold for a perfectly matched repair.

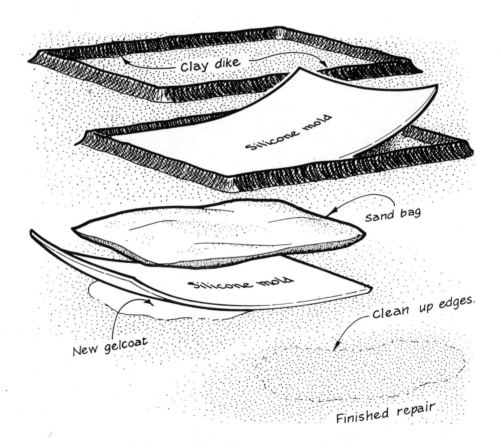

Clay dike

Silicone mold

sand bag

Silicone mold

New gelcoat

clean up edges.

Finished repair.

SEALING YOUR SEALANT

With the high cost of some sealants, adhesives, and bedding compounds that are packaged in cylinders, it makes a lot of sense to preserve what remains in the tube after you have finished a current job. Being able to seal your sealant will also assure that it will remain in a usable state until the next time you need it.

John Iannacone from Tulsa, Oklahoma, who sails a Catalina 22 called *Ten Grand*, suggests two methods that not only serve these objectives but also prevent the sealant from continuing to ooze out once you've finished using it. Release the pressure in the cylinder by turning and then retracting the ramrod, then insert a tight-fit, small-diameter bolt into the spigot hole. Screw the bolt all the way in for long-term preservation. An alternative to the bolt is to screw a large-diameter electrical wire nut onto the end of the spigot.

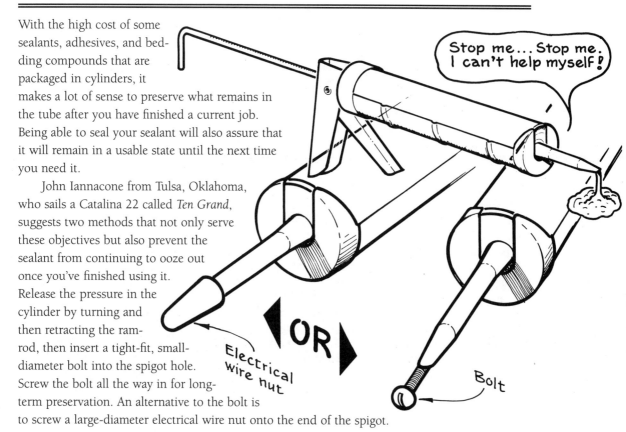

INSTALLING SCREWS IN THIN MATERIAL

Attaching shelving, brackets, or lightly loaded hardware to thin structures such as icebox interiors, headliners, and laminated panels can pose a problem, particularly if it's impossible to use bolts and nuts. And tapping thin materials to receive machine screws is rarely successful, as Michael Murray found out while trying to install a freezer unit aboard *At Ease II*. His solution was to push correctly sized plastic inserts into drill holes to receive screws or bolts. The inserts are the same kind normally used for fastening into drywall.

177